Titles in Contributions in Military Studies

CURRENT FRENCH SE
POLICY

Current French Security Policy

THE GAULLIST LEGACY

Theodore Robert Posner

CONTRIBUTIONS IN MILITARY STUDIES,
NUMBER 118
Colin Gray, *Series Adviser*

GREENWOOD PRESS

New York • Westport, Connecticut • London

Library of Congress Cataloging-in-Publication Data

Posner, Theodore Robert.
   Current French security policy : the Gaullist legacy / Theodore
Robert Posner.
      p.   cm.—(Contributions in military studies, ISSN 0883–6884
; no. 118)
   Includes bibliographical references and index.
   ISBN 0–313–27934–9 (alk. paper)
   1. France—Military policy.   2. France—Military relations.
3. Europe—Military relations.   4. Europe—National security.
I. Title. II. Series.
UA700.P66   1991
355′.0335′44—dc20   91–21195

British Library Cataloguing in Publication Data is available.

Library of Congress Catalog Card Number: 91–21195
ISBN: 0–313–27934–9
ISSN: 0883–6884

First published in 1991

Greenwood Press, 88 Post Road West, Westport, CT   06881
An imprint of Greenwood Publishing Group, Inc.

Printed in the United States of America

The paper used in this book complies with the
Permanent Paper Standard issued by the National
Information Standards Organization (Z39.48–1984).

10 9 8 7 6 5 4 3 2 1

To my mother.

CONTENTS

PREFACE

Europe in the aftermath of the Cold War, while seemingly less war-prone, is much more complex than cold war Europe. One learns little about the state of Europe today by restricting one's view primarily to the foreign policies of the two superpowers. The observation that the dissolution of blocs staring each other down at the center of the continent has upset the basic assumptions of forty years has become commonplace. But what does that observation mean for the study of current security policy in Europe?

For some it means turning to new security problems, such as drug trade and terrorism. For others it means looking anew at what were once considered by many to be ineffective institutions, such as the Conference on Security and Cooperation in Europe. And for still others it means reexamining the influence and responsibilities of state actors that played secondary roles next to the United States and the Soviet Union during the Cold War. This last purpose is the goal of the present work.

France, since the end of the Second World War, has sought persistently to reestablish its rank in the world. A permanent seat in the Security Council of the United Nations and an independent nuclear force were steps in the right direction, but neither of these could prevent the United States and Soviet Union from determining the shape of security relations in Europe. From his return to power in 1958, President Charles de Gaulle tried to lay down an alternative basis of security, distinct from the foundation built by the superpowers. To France's Western European partners he presented a framework of cooperative security which challenged the model preferred by the United States within the Atlantic Alliance. While de Gaulle's challenge was substantial, the circumstances of the Cold War favored American leadership in the West.

Those circumstances were overturned by the spread of democracy in the countries of Eastern and Central Europe since 1989. The givens of a new era warrant a reevaluation of the Gaullist model for security, which never got off the ground in the 1960s, though at times it appeared to come close. The present work is an analysis of that model and of the possibility that France, a state that played a second-rank role in a bipolar world, might play a first-rank role in a multipolar world.

I would like to thank Professor Richard Ullman for his help and guidance. I am also grateful to the staff and directors of The National Security Archive, whose assistance was important in compiling documents for the historical sections of this work.

CURRENT FRENCH SECURITY POLICY

INTRODUCTION

France's role and rank on the world stage, and especially in Europe, the cornerstone in the Gaullist foundation of the Fifth Republic, gained new relevance amidst the upheaval which shook Europe beginning in the autumn of 1989. While the sudden end of the Cold War provoked a flood of new questions, it also re-opened old ones, amongst which were the division of privileges and responsibilities of leadership in western security. A rapidly diminishing threat from the East, capped by the dissolution of the Warsaw Pact as a military entity, has paved the way for a new debate on security cooperation in Europe. Therein lies the possibility for realization of the legacy of General Charles de Gaulle. While the rhetoric of France's role and rank in European security, as in other domains, has hardly abated since de Gaulle, the end of the Cold War has provided a new opportunity to translate role and rank into concrete policy.

To understand this opportunity, it is interesting to look back at a historical analogy to the emerging political order. The revolutionary transformation of Europe has sent scholars and statesmen alike scrambling for the most appropriate such comparisons. Did 1990 most closely resemble 1914, when rising nationalism sparked fundamental shifts in the international system? Or is the inter-war period, when the permanence of peace seemed certain, the more relevant model? The apparent dismantling of superpower politics, signaling a return to multipolarity in Europe, has prompted some observers to reexamine the restoration of a concert of Europe following the Congress of Vienna in 1815.[1]

The shift toward multipolarity, acute sensitivity to the burden of military costs, and the pressing nature of domestic issues suggest, albeit at an abstract level, similarities to Europe in the aftermath of the Napoleonic wars.[2] Henry Kissinger's assessment of the "world restored" at the Congress of Vienna might describe equally well Europe 175 years later. "The problem," in both periods, "was to create an order in which change could be brought about through a sense of obligation, instead of through an assertion of power."[3] This ideal would seem to be in the spirit of the much-invoked, if much less defined, "new world order" of the cold war aftermath. The analogy highlights France's potential role as the influential "balancer" in the new order.

Just as in 1815 France had joined the great powers at Vienna in order to balance the territorial interests of Prussia and Russia with those of Great Britain and Austria, so today France has sought to reinvigorate strong working relationships with both Germany and the Soviet Union in an effort to reconcile old differences in the interest of a new order.

A rekindled and carefully nurtured friendship with Bonn has been an important theme of President François Mitterrand's foreign policy. Formalized in 1982 by reactivation of the 1963 Elysée Treaty—the basis of the special relationship between France and Germany—security cooperation between the two countries increased over the course of the decade and into the 1990s. At the same time, an identifiable Paris-Moscow link is evolving. Supporters point to Mitterrand's early and unwavering confidence in Mikhail Gorbachev's leadership.[4] The French president's visit to Kiev in December 1989, during which he and Gorbachev exchanged common views on German unification and the idea of holding a Conference on Security and Cooperation in Europe (CSCE) heads of state summit in 1990, may have given a new impetus to that relationship.[5] At one extreme, some have even alluded to a future Franco-Soviet alliance, forged from common fear of an overpowering Germany.[6] While France is unlikely to go that far, its position as balancer between a strong Germany and a still imposing, although somewhat weakened, Soviet Union bears striking resemblance to its position in 1815, which hints at the potential influence France might exercise. Regulating, to the extent possible, the pace of change in Europe, the Paris-Bonn "accelerator" and the Paris-Moscow "brake" could become important mechanisms for controlling the form and content of a new, multipolar security order.

Statements by French political leaders reflect an appreciation of France's unique geopolitical position in the emerging European order. The chairman of the Defense Commission of the French National Assembly, Jean-Michel Boucheron, observed in December 1989, "Everyone is assessing, at the moment, the critical role that this situation will confer on France."[7] Addressing the Institut des hautes études de défense nationale in May 1990, former Prime Minister Jacques Chirac observed, "The United States and France are the only countries that can pretend to share the formidable responsibility of the rebalanced Alliance of tomorrow."[8] From late 1989 until his resignation in January 1991, Defense Minister Jean-Pierre Chevènement promoted "the progressive building of a European identity in security" with a clear emphasis on the leading role France's political and military contributions would play in this direction.[9]

These expressions of a more vital French role in post-cold war European security became more pronounced in May and June 1991, as NATO defense and foreign ministers set out to reshape the Alliance for a new era. This period, only a few months after the U.S.-led victory in the war to expel Iraq from Kuwait, was marked by two important meetings. First, a conference of defense ministers in Brussels (28–29 May) approved plans to reorganize NATO ground forces into multinational corps, including a special rapid reaction force. One week later, in Copenhagen, foreign ministers began to put into place the pieces of NATO's future agenda.

On both occasions Paris set itself apart from the dominant American vision of security, and this had a significant impact. While France did not participate in the Brussels meeting, (as it has remained outside the Alliance's integrated military structure since 1966), both the Foreign Minister and President Mitterrand raised objections to the newly-created multinational corps and emphasized that French troops would not be part of these units.[10] Those statements had the important effect of reminding Europe that the NATO defense ministers' communiqué would not be the final word in security organization. Indeed, as one commentary noted, "Until the issue of Europe's future defense identity is settled, NATO will remain a lame animal, whatever the new structure of its forces."[11] Clearly, that identity will not be defined without or against France, as Foreign Minister Roland Dumas made known at the Copenhagen conference.

The NATO foreign ministers' communiqué of 6 June bore the distinct marks of French influence. For the first time, an official NATO document acknowledged the competence of the European Community in the area of security, despite memoranda which Washington had sent to EC states warning against the formation of a new European security organization.[12] Achieving this recognition, France ensured that NATO initiatives will not block progress in the EC's intergovernmental conference on political integration, which is trying to develop a common European security policy. France also contested proposals to make NATO the primary forum for stronger East-West cooperation and persuaded the foreign ministers to acknowledge the role of the Conference on Security and Cooperation in Europe as well in this area. Thus, France successfully exercised its leverage at this key moment in constructing a new European order. It effectively intervened to prevent the new wine of security from being poured into old bottles.

Support for strong French leadership in a new Europe preceded the historical watershed of 1989. The momentum behind this idea increased throughout the 1980s.[13] One of its most notable exponents has been former West German Chancellor Helmut Schmidt, who in 1987 speculated that "Europe's self-assertion will largely depend on whether and how France is to play a leading role."[14] More recently, Christian Democratic leader Alfred Dregger noted that current changes demand of the Atlantic Alliance "a European strategy and an American strategy, such that Europeans would be on equal footing with Americans, in particular in command structures. *It is here that France has a role to play*" (my emphasis).[15] The unraveling of European political systems in 1989 did not give birth to the idea of strong French leadership in a new security order, but it did elevate the possibility to a qualitatively new level.

OVERCOMING INSTITUTIONAL INERTIA

Until the autumn of 1989, serious consideration of alternative frameworks for European security had been precluded by the remarkable degree of inertia entrenched in the institutional policy-making mechanisms of the North Atlantic Treaty Organization. Conventional force levels, argues analyst John Duffield, were a good indicator of this inertia.[16] While profound changes in the international structure over forty years might have increased the expectation of equally profound shifts in the Alliance's force posture, the staying power of force planning and other decision-making processes preempted such responses. Thus, for instance, NATO's level of conventional armament largely did not reflect either the warming of East-West relations in the late 1960s or the buildup of Soviet military power during the 1970s. As Duffield notes, "Increasingly, institutional inertia and constraints have tended to prevail over structural pressures for change." "When," he asks, "does an institution become so out of line with the underlying power structure that it must change?"[17] The unfolding of events in Europe since 1989 suggests one answer.

The unprecedented willingness of the Soviet Union to draw down military forces, as demonstrated in the Conventional Forces in Europe (CFE) Treaty and in unilateral initiatives, popular revolutions throughout Eastern Europe, and the crumbling of the Warsaw Pact, have created immense pressure on NATO to relax its own force posture. Indeed, individual Alliance members, such as Belgium and the Netherlands, announced as early as January 1990 plans to withdraw forces unilaterally, according to their perceptions of a permanently receding threat from the East.[18] Today, military reductions in the West are announced faster than NATO institutions can digest and analyze their implications.

Inevitably, drastically lower force levels will require reconsideration of the strategic underpinnings of Alliance security. New strategy, in turn, will probably lead to new decision-making mechanisms and more fundamental alterations in the concept of European security. In other words, the events since 1989 have induced a reversal in the Alliance planning process. The accustomed progression from broad goals to strategy to operational force posture would appear to have been weakened by rapid structural change. Instead, forces are being reduced before leaders can consider carefully and come to agreement on the corresponding broad visions.

This reversal of process was evident in NATO's decision to reorganize ground forces, as described above. Efficiency may demand smaller forces, emphasizing, as Alliance officials have stated, "mobility, flexibility, and multinationality."[19] But beyond assurances that the new multinational corps would be used to counter an ill-defined threat called "uncertainty," the decision to reshuffle NATO's force structures was not accompanied by a corresponding, clearly articulated broad vision or strategy. This explains speculation in 1990 and 1991 about the circumstances in which NATO units might be employed in the future. NATO troops will conduct more mobility-oriented maneuvers—which will require more space, a consequence that will not be well received in German towns and villages—yet, for the moment, the broader picture remains blurry at best.

One might draw from this reversal the following hypothesis: The key link in the interaction between structural and institutional trends is the rate of change. In the case of European security, structural pressures began to overcome institutional inertia when the rate of shifts in the former were too rapid for the latter to respond in its accustomed manner. The relative incoherence of response, in turn, has begun to cripple NATO institutions. Past alterations of the foundation of East-West relations were profound, but they transpired slowly enough for Alliance institutions to adapt. While the alarmingly fast pace of today's structural transition has not yet uprooted the institutions of West European security, it has raised fundamental questions about the future.

These questions may temporarily be put on hold because of the impact in the West of the rapid and efficient American-led success in undoing Iraq's invasion of Kuwait in the first months of 1991. The strong impression left by the seven-month affair has certainly given many countries pause to reconsider security needs in the post–cold war era. In the West, obstacles to a coordinated European military policy in the Gulf (with the possible exception of naval operations) combined with a new European appreciation for the value of the American contribution to security may have halted institutional change in the Atlantic alliance and of Europe's security for the moment. That this should be the case was evidently the message implied in warnings sent by an American undersecretary of state to European leaders in April 1991. The notes advised, in "harsh terms," against initiatives toward creation of a European defense establishment that might weaken NATO.[20] NATO's ministerial meetings of late May and early June were described as "more remarkable for what [they] preserved of NATO than for what [they] changed . . . "[21] By drawing attention away from Western Europe, the Gulf crisis may have allowed policy-makers the time to consider necessary institutional reform in the Alliance without the pressure of the international spotlight. Nevertheless, American force reductions in Europe did continue, even during the Persian Gulf war, and while the

United States will probably benefit for a while from strengthened clout within the Alliance, fast-paced structural change in European security is ultimately likely to dominate.

Looking beyond the immediate aftershocks of the Persian Gulf crisis, the rate of structural change in Europe is approaching the point where it may set in motion a bottom-up transformation of security institutions. The traditional top-down process, by which strategic and political goals determined force levels, is being reversed, and the division of responsibilities and privileges in European security is bound, therefore, to change. The purpose of this analysis is to try to understand the implications of the current transformation for the future leadership and shape of institutions in European security, looking ahead, specifically, to the potential for a strong French influence.

The reader may wonder at this focus on France during a period in which united Germany enjoys pride of place in Europe. In fact, it is precisely because Germany finds itself in a position at once powerful and delicate that it may be less likely than France to take initiative in the area of security. German leaders are conscious of their country's history and sensitive to concerns that other countries will have following unification. They are also aware of the leading role Germany will inevitably play in the fields of trade and finance. There would be little reason to spoil this advantage by provoking the fears likely to arise were Germany to exert too strong an influence over European security. By virtue of size and geography Germany will automatically have an important impact on the institutions and decision-making processes of a new security order. However, it is less likely than France to assert strongly its vision of that order.

As cited above, there are some German statesmen who actively support a strong French leadership in European security (e.g., Schmidt and Dregger). Furthermore, Germans demonstrated their aversion toward things military during the war in the Persian Gulf. Official vacillation in material support for the anti-Iraq coalition and popular pacifism marked Germany's stand on post–cold war security matters. One can by no means say that Germany has bowed out of the defense field, but policy leadership would seem to be left to others, and first, France.

Driven by lower force levels, a rethinking of the institutional bases of European security will provide France with the opportunity to assert its distinct concept of cooperative security among sovereign states.

Assuredly, force levels are not the only determinant of leadership in
Europe. Indeed, it would be impossible to study force levels in a vacuum,
ignoring the awesome political changes taking place in Central Europe,
the Soviet Union, and Germany. However, it is possible to isolate
force levels as the most observable medium through which political
transformations in Europe are absorbed and transmitted. While not the
sole cause behind shifts in leadership (they are at once a cause and
an effect), force levels do have a profound impact, and they are clear
indicators of such shifts.

FORCE LEVELS AND ALLIANCE LEADERSHIP

Major watersheds in NATO's history have been demarcated by the
nature of forces in being. American predominance in the early history
of the Alliance, for example, was clearly a function of, at first, the
American monopoly in nuclear weapons, and later, the possession of
intercontinental ballistic missiles. The ultimate protection which the
nuclear umbrella provided Europe confirmed American leadership.

During the 1960s, American encouragement of greater reliance on
conventional weapons, combined with the deployment of tactical nuclear
weapons in Europe, shifted the balance of influence in NATO more
toward Europe. States with American nuclear weapons based on their
soil, most notably the Federal Republic of Germany (FRG), now had
a new source of leverage vis-à-vis Washington. Furthermore, pressure
for improved conventional defense raised doubts about the commitment
of the United States to extended deterrence. The physical presence of
American troops in Europe had become a *quid pro quo* for American
leadership in European security. In 1967, asked whether a token force of
two divisions would be sufficient to achieve American objectives, acting
Secretary of State Nicholas Katzenbach responded that such a reduction
"would change the whole basis of our relationship with Europe and of
the Alliance."[22]

Duffield observes that the years following President Kennedy's
assassination "were largely devoted simply to holding the Alliance
together."[23] It was this transformation in intra-Alliance relations that
facilitated the debate between France and the United States, which we
will examine, over formal arrangements for the defense of Western
Europe. The various dilemmas were closely connected to the nature

and level of forces in Europe. The most apparent outcome of this watershed was the institutionalization of highly integrative decision-making mechanisms, which cushioned any further change.

By extension, then, reductions in force levels, pursuant to the Conventional Forces in Europe agreement and future accords, will be a critical link in the current transformation of leadership in European security. To reiterate, this will not be the sole cause of change. Drastically lower force levels will reflect significant institutional changes and will further catalyze the process of change.

SIGNS OF TRANSITION IN THE ATLANTIC ALLIANCE

The necessary conditions for a critical reexamination of the American-led structure of European security have been falling into place over the past decade; extremely low force levels would be the last straw in the transition. American policy initiatives in the 1980s, including the Strategic Defense Initiative (SDI), the Follow-on Forces Attack (FOFA) strategic subconcept for NATO, the "double zero" option for intermediate-range nuclear force reductions, and the modernization of short-range nuclear weapons, sparked intense criticism in Europe of U.S. leadership. While the United States was able to absorb these blows through the mechanisms of Alliance policy-making, their effect set in motion a slow erosion of American leadership, which the American-led victory in the Persian Gulf war may have halted only temporarily.

The unveiling of SDI in 1983 prompted extensive questioning of American leadership. A report to Congress in 1987 found that Europeans generally perceived SDI as an instance of "American insensitivity and lack of commitment to the future of extended deterrence."[24] Deep concerns inspired by the concept of a nuclear umbrella over the United States were exacerbated by the awkward manner in which other NATO members were invited to participate in the project. (As if presenting ultimata, the U.S. Department of Defense had required each country to strike a separate agreement of cooperation with the United States within sixty days of the offer.)[25]

European Alliance partners also responded skeptically to the American presentation of Follow-on Forces Attack in the mid-1980s. This operational concept called for incorporation into NATO defense plans of the capability to launch precision interdiction strikes against secondary and tertiary echelons of a Warsaw Pact attack against the West. The concept drew on developments in a vast array of emerging high technology target acquisition capabilities, weapons platforms, and munitions. Europeans saw FOFA as too costly, and some, particularly political parties on the Left, criticized the plan for its inherently offensive character. FOFA was, in fact, adopted by NATO as an operational concept in November 1984, but it was placed on a very low level of priority.

Perhaps the greatest watershed for the erosion of U.S. leadership in the 1980s, prior to the spring of 1989, was the Reagan-Gorbachev Reykjavik summit of October 1986. United States agreement to the elimination of intermediate-range nuclear forces in Europe, without first consulting the other NATO Allies, confirmed Europeans' worst nightmares of superpower domination of their security interests. One observer describes the reaction of the French to Reykjavik as strikingly similar to their reaction to the Suez Crisis thirty years earlier, the decisive moment in French realization of weakened status next to two nuclear superpowers. Both events had an "enormous impact on foreign policy."[26]

Less than three years after Reykjavik, the United States came under attack again in Western Europe for its initial insistence on modernizing the Lance short-range nuclear missile. The debate on that issue, which erupted in February 1989 when West German Chancellor Helmut Kohl announced his view that NATO need not make an early decision on Lance's fate,[27] truly put American influence to the test. In the weeks following Kohl's announcement, indication of Belgian and Danish support for the German position clearly marked the fault lines within the Alliance. From the American and British point of view, the idea of a "third zero" (i.e., the elimination of short-range nuclear weapons) would constitute an abandonment of the Alliance's strategy of flexible response, an essential basis of American leadership. While a compromise solution was eventually reached, whereby negotiations on reduction of short-range nuclear forces would be deferred until agreement on conventional force reduction was completed, provided that future nuclear reduction talks not lead to a third zero, American leverage was damaged in the struggle.

Resounding victory in the Gulf war of 1991 will undoubtedly forestall erosion of American leadership in European security. Iraq's invasion of

Kuwait (not to mention the Soviet Union's inclination to use military force to suppress independence movements in the Baltic republics while the rest of the world was preoccupied with the crisis in the Middle East) has reminded Europe that the world may not yet be as safe as it seemed to be in 1990. According to one European official in NATO, the Iraq crisis "has demonstrated the limits of European power, and it has shown that only the United States can play the role of global policeman."[28]

However, even during the crisis the European structural change of the 1980s that accelerated from 1989 continued apace, highlighted by formal dissolution of the Warsaw Pact as a military entity. Accordingly, while the United States was sending soldiers to Saudi Arabia, it was also continuing plans to reduce its presence in Western Europe, and of the more than 150,000 American soldiers sent from Europe to the Middle East, many may not be returned to their original assignments.[29] Although the Gulf crisis reaffirmed the importance of the American contribution to western security, it did not overturn the long-term trend in Europe. Whereas in response to the jolt of political, structural change, American force levels initially leapfrogged over broad goals for European security, the former becoming the determinant of the latter, broad goals must ultimately fall into line, as must decision-making institutions.

If leadership in European security becomes an open question, the French factor will take on new importance. By withdrawing from NATO's integrated military structure in 1966, France relinquished its opportunity to play a leading role. A major shift in force levels may afford it a new occasion to reassert its concept of European security—a concept which contrasts fundamentally with the American concept.

FRANCE'S NEW OPPORTUNITY

The value to overall European security of French military forces, territorial depth, and logistical support could grow immensely, pursuant to a massive reduction of American troops and support. France's assets would take on a formerly unrealized significance. In an interview in July 1990, then Defense Minister Jean-Pierre Chevènement acknowledged the growing importance of military status as an instrument of political leverage: "The credibility of [French] diplomacy depends more on the independent military capacity we have given ourselves than on our export capacity or our seat in the Security Council."[30] Similarly, former Prime Minister Jacques Chirac noted, "It is precisely by the standard of our conventional forces that our European allies, notably the Germans, measure the sincerity of our solidarity and, therefore, our political influence too, at a decisive moment for the redefinition of the European security system."[31] These statements are representative of the tenor of one current dialogue in France.

Given that French military capability will *de facto* loom larger in Europe as superpower forces are drawn down, it is possible to see how French influence in designing the new political architecture on the continent could grow commensurately. The logic in this conclusion may be difficult to grasp at first, as one might expect that the end of the Cold War, the waning legitimacy of armed might as an accepted currency of inter-state relations, and the disappearance of any clear threat to European security would weaken the political leverage formerly associated with military power. However, as will be argued, the import- ance which Europeans, and policy-makers in particular, attach to military capability is likely to remain high for the foreseeable future. Even as the Cold War fades, the value of the military dimension of security will be bolstered by entrenched ways of thinking coupled with a sense that the ability to muster an armed defense is reassuring even when a potential enemy is not in sight. The two events that broke the initial post– cold war euphoria—Iraq's invasion of Kuwait and the Soviet Union's use of force in the Baltic republics—will reenforce these themes. If the military dimension of security is still valued, then France will face an opportunity to move into a privileged position in European security.

THE MECHANISMS OF SECURITY LEADERSHIP

The increased influence that France would gain pursuant to a substan- tial American withdrawal from the continent would be reflected in the new or reshaped institutions of European security. It is through various institutional forms that one can see how the United States has exercised responsibility and control in NATO during the Alliance's forty years. That is what is meant by leadership in security. A brief survey of the policy-making mechanisms of American leadership should signal where to look for indications of emerging French leadership.

Today's peacetime force planning incorporates the American preference for tight-knit integration within the Alliance, in contrast to the French preference for looser cooperation. (The historical basis and continued relevance of this basic conceptual difference will be analyzed later in this volume.) Beginning in the mid-1960s, American statesmen, most important among them Secretary of Defense McNamara, realized that the United States, rather than insisting on particular force contributions from individual allies, could more effectively achieve its goals by "seeking procedural and organizational innovations," which would assure the establishment of constant benchmark force levels.[32] At McNamara's urging, NATO adopted in December 1966 a force planning procedure that would combine the guidance of political as well as military leaders. It was hoped that by adopting this regular procedure, member countries would feel a stronger obligation to fulfill the force commitments agreed to in each plan. Formerly, force goals had been based exclusively on military guidance and were so out of sync with available assets that they often went unfulfilled.[33] By establishing a regular procedure, the United States ensured close integration in actual peacetime force planning rather than hollow promises from individual allies.

American influence in this process increased during the 1970s with development of the NATO Long Term Defense Plan (LTDP), which grew out of U.S. Defense Department study AD-80. The proposals of AD-80 included "broadening NATO defense planning to cover overall defense resource allocation," establishing a longer time frame for defense planning, and adopting "stronger multinational funding mechanisms." The nine task forces assigned to implement those concepts through NATO's LTDP were usually marked by a strong American presence, and, in contrast to formal NATO consultative fora, did not always operate on the basis of unanimity.[34]

American leadership in western security is further reflected in the threat assessment process. Naturally, an essential component of force planning is intelligence on the potential adversary's capabilities and intentions. In this area–the complex technology and processes of intelligence gathering and dissemination–the United States has established a virtual monopoly. While there are two parallel threat assessment mechanisms in the West, one using American and the other using

Alliance intelligence, the former would seem to dominate. Testifying before the Senate Armed Services Committee in 1987, the Director of Intelligence, U.S. European Command, commented, "It is a recognized advantage . . . in NATO that the U.S. intelligence collection network is the largest and the most productive." He then pointed out the problems of communications which can obstruct sharing that intelligence with other NATO members.[35] American control over this critical function in turn provides leverage for the United States to influence force planning and strategic deliberations.

Another set of institutional mechanisms that embodies U.S. leadership and the American concept of Alliance integration is arms control. Since the Cuban Missile Crisis, Michael Stürmer explains, "by and large, Europeans have left arms control to the U.S. negotiating teams."[36] Under U.S. leadership, NATO has developed not only tools for crisis and wartime planning, but also those for negotiating a stable peace. The Partial Test Ban Treaty, the Nuclear Non-Proliferation Treaty, and various other agreements to which NATO states are party have been negotiated with the United States essentially representing the West. That relationship was challenged in the first round of the Conventional Forces in Europe talks. Specifically, France's strong objections to a bloc-to-bloc approach to those negotiations may have been the most tangible harbinger up to that moment of shifts in the institutional foundations of European security.

In the aftermath of the Persian Gulf crisis, France made another bid to lead the way in arms control. It offered, as a "complement" to the American plan for arms control in the Middle East, a broader project for global arms control, to include both suppliers and buyers. As part of the proposal, the French offered to sign the Nuclear Non-Proliferation Treaty of 1968, which they had followed *de facto*, though they had not adhered to it *de jure*. This important step indicated France's will to enhance its credibility as a leader in arms control and, in turn, in European security. "France would thus confirm its initiative," according to three experts in international relations, "as nation and as principal partner in the European Community, in the construction of a new, more stable, more peaceful international order . . . "[37]

Competing American and French visions of the future of arms control illustrate that institutional manifestations of arms control are a critical repository of leadership in a European security order. One observer notes that "disarmament has become the privileged mechanism of change in

East-West relations."[38] Developments in this area, as in the areas of threat assessment and force planning, will be important indicators of changing leadership relationships in European security.

NOTES

1. The relevance of 1815 as a model for current policy-making was suggested persuasively to me by Dr. Wolfgang Danspeckgruber.

2. Clifford A. Kupchan and Charles A. Kupchan, "After NATO: Concert of Europe," *The New York Times*, 6 July 1990, p. A25.

3. Henry A. Kissinger, *A World Restored* (Gloucester, MA, Peter Smith, 1973), p. 172.

4. Jean-Marie Colombani and Jean-Yves Lhomeau, "Le sens d'un septennat," *Le Monde*, 16 November 1989, p. 10. The authors maintain that Mitterrand was one of the first western leaders to express his confidence that Gorbachev would encourage fundamental change in Eastern Europe.

5. Jacques Amalric, "Bonn fait une concession importante," *Le Monde*, 8 December 1989, pp. 1–2.

6. David S. Yost, "France in the New Europe," *Foreign Affairs* (Winter, 1990/91), p. 126.

7. Jean-Michel Boucheron, "Accélérer le désarmement classique," *Le Monde*, 2 December 1989, p. 2. In similar fashion, the former chairman of the committee, François Fillon, wrote, "France, the only western continental power possessing nuclear arms, is in a position to play a central role in building a [Western European security] community." See François Fillon, "François Mitterrand a dégagé en touche," *Le Monde*, 26 May 1989, p. 2.

8. "M. Chirac favorable à des unités multinationales sous commandement européen," *Le Monde*, 25 May 1990, p. 7. Former President Valery Giscard d'Estaing has similarly stated that in exchange for measures to calm German concerns about prestrategic nuclear weapons use, Germany "must accept that France may exercise certain responsibilities of command in Europe." See "M. Giscard d'Estaing souhaite 'une solidarité' franco-allemande en matière de défense," *Le Monde*, 3 April 1990, p. 3.

9. "M. Chevènement plaide pour une 'identité européene' en matière de sécurité," *Le Monde*, 7 December 1989, p. 3. See also Jacques Isnard, "Un entretien avec M. Chevènement," *Le Monde*, 13 July 1990, p. 9.

10. David White, "NATO Plans Rapid Reaction Force Commanded by UK," *The Financial Times*, 31 May 1991, p. 1. And, William Drozdiak, "Paris and Bonn Want Gorbachev at G-7 Summit," *The International Herald Tribune*, 31 May 1991, pp. 1, 5.

11. "Nato's New Structure," *The Financial Times*, 30 May 1991, p. 18.

12. See extracts from communiqué in *Le Monde*, 10 June 1991, p. 3. On memoranda sent by the United States to EC states, see Flora Lewis, "America Could Leave the Pedestal Gracefully," *The International Herald Tribune*, 19 April 1991, p. 6.

13. Anton W. DePorte, "French Security Policy in Its Domestic and International Settings," in Philippe G. Le Prestre, ed., *French Security Policy in a Disarming World* (Boulder, CO, Lynne Rienner Publishers, 1989), p. 2.

14. Helmut Schmidt, "Europe Should Begin to Assert Itself, and the French Should Take the Lead," article from *Die Zeit* translated in *World Press Review* (February 1987), p. 23.

See also Barry Blechman and Cathleen Fischer, "West German Security Policy and the Franco-German Relationship," in Robbin F. Laird, ed., *Strangers and Friends: The Franco-German Security Relationship* (London, Pinter Publishers, 1989), pp. 63–64.

15. Cited in André Giraud, "Construction européene et défense," *Politique Étrangère* (no. 3, 1990), p. 518.

16. John Stuart Duffield, "The Evolution of NATO's Conventional Force Posture" (Ph.D. Dissertation, Princeton University, 1989), p. 529.

17. Duffield, p. 536.

18. Christian Chartier, "La Belgique et les Pays-Bas annoncent une réduction de leurs troupes stationnées en RFA," *Le Monde*, 27 January 1990, p. 4.

19. Barbara Starr, "Cold War Battle Orders Make Way for a New NATO Era," *Jane's Defense Weekly*, 8 June 1991, p. 96.

20. Flora Lewis, "America Could Leave the Pedestal Gracefully," *The International Herald Tribune*, 19 April 1991, p. 6.

21. NATO officials, cited in Joseph Fitchett, "Postwar U.S. Ascendancy Sidetracks Europe's Aspirations," *The International Herald Tribune*, 12 June 1991, p. 5.

22. Testimony of Hon. Nicholas deB. Katzenbach in U.S. Congress, Senate, Combined Subcommittee of Foreign Relations and Armed Services Committees on the Subject of United States Troops in Europe, *United States Troops in Europe*, Hearing before the Combined Subcommittee of Foreign Relations and Armed Services Committees on the Subject of United States Troops in Europe, 90th Cong., 1st Sess., 26 April; 3 May 1967, p. 46.

23. Duffield, p. 318.

24. U.S. Congress, House, Committee on Foreign Affairs, Subcommittee on Europe and the Middle East, *Challenges to NATO's Consensus: West European Attitudes and U.S. Policy*, Report prepared by Foreign Affairs and National Defense Division, Congressional Research Service, 100th Cong., 1st Sess., 1987.

25. John Fenske, "France and the Strategic Defense Initiative: Speeding Up or Putting on the Brakes?" *International Affairs* (Spring, 1986), p. 235.

26. Philippe G. Le Prestre, "The Lessons of Cohabitation," in Le Prestre, ed., p. 25.

27. David Marsh, "Kohl Rejects Early Missile Replacement," *Financial Times*, 10 February 1989, p. 18.

28. Cited in Alan Riding, "Allies Reminded of Need for U.S. Shield," *The New York Times*, 12 August 1990, p. A14.

29. Eric Schmitt, "Army Is Paring Its Forces Despite Buildup in Gulf," *The New York Times*, 21 September 1990, p. A9. See also Edouard Balladur, "Pour une nouvelle politique de défense," *Le Monde*, 6 March 1991, p. 2. In a report presented to President Bush in June 1990, the U.S. Defense Department outlined strategic concepts for the 1990s that included manpower cuts of 500,000 and consideration of reduction of forces stationed in Europe to between 100,000 and 125,000. More important than the numbers themselves, the "blueprint" represented a first effort toward linking broad goals and force postures, corresponding to profound change in the European political context. See Michael R. Gordon, "Pentagon Drafts Strategy for Post–Cold War World," *The New York Times*, 2 August 1990, pp. 1, 4.

30. Cited in Jacques Isnard, "Un entretien avec M. Chevènement," *Le Monde*, 13 July 1990, p. 9. In December 1989 Chevènement observed that "the credibility of its military force is probably, today, one of the great sources of leverage that France has in organizing European security." Cited in Jérôme Dumoulin and Sylvie Pierre-Brossolette, "Chevènement: La réunification n'est pas d'actualité," *L'Express* (24 November 1989), p. 30.

31. Jacques Chirac, "Une remise en cause insidieuse de notre défense," *Le Monde*, 10 June 1989, p. 18.

32. Duffield, p. 423.

33. Duffield, pp. 395–96.

34. Duffield, pp. 463 (quote), 467, 482.

35. Major General C. Norman Wood, Director of Intelligence, U.S. European Command, in U.S. Congress, Senate, Committee on Armed Services, Subcommittee on Conventional Forces and Alliance Defense, *Alliance and Defense Capabilities in Europe*, Hearing before the Subcommittee on Conventional Forces and Alliance Defense, 100th Cong., 1st Sess., 4 August; 7, 20 October; 3, 17 November 1987, p. 58. Elaboration on difficulties of sharing intelligence was deleted.

36. Michael Stürmer, "Is NATO Still in Europe's Interest?" in Stanley R. Sloan, ed., *NATO in the 1990s* (Washington, D.C., Pergamon-Brassey's, 1989), p. 116.

37. Karl Kaiser, Laurence Martin, Cesare Merlini, "La France devrait adhérer au traité de non-prolifération," *Le Monde*, 3 June 1991, p. 2.

38. Claire Tréan, "Calmer le jeu par le désarmement," *Le Monde*, 2 December 1989, p. 1.

CHAPTER 1

INTEGRATION VERSUS COOPERATION: THE HISTORICAL DEBATE

A political transformation of the magnitude foreseeable in modern-day Europe prompts an examination of historical points of reference. For NATO, the last major debate on fundamental defense issues unfolded over the period from 1963 to 1967. During those years, France and the United States presented Western Europe with two diametrically opposed visions of the Alliance.[1] The former, under the presidency of Charles de Gaulle, proposed a loosely connected cooperative organization of sovereign nations committed to the simple but firm pledge that each would consider an attack on any other as an attack on itself. The United States, by contrast, proposed a tightly integrated organization committed not only to a pledge of mutual defense, but also to coordination of peacetime force planning and military production, economic cooperation, and political unity. The French concept will be referred to as *cooperation* and the American concept as *integration*.

The efforts of each country to press for its preferred vision may be seen as a competition to win a privileged position of leadership in European security, the reward being the opportunity to shape the institutions of a security order according to the winner's broad vision. The competition was temporarily put to rest in 1966, following France's withdrawal from the Alliance's integrated military command and NATO's subsequent adoption of flexible response doctrine. Today, the extremely rapid rate of structural change in European security relationships may cause the fundamental debate to be replayed in the 1990s.

Studying the dynamics of the earlier competition should provide considerable insight into the dimensions likely to evolve in the new debate. If it can then be demonstrated that today either the United States or France has a greater degree of leverage and that it would exercise that leverage in pursuit of its historical goals, it should be possible to make some general forecasts as to the future shape of European security.

DEFINING THE DEBATE

At the foundation of West European security, the very text of the North Atlantic Treaty incorporates a bias toward close-knit integration—the American philosophy. Even before mentioning mutual defense (article five), the Treaty mandates "continuous and effective self-help and mutual aid" (article three) and calls on all parties "to eliminate conflict in their international economic policies and to encourage economic collaboration between any or all of them" (article two).[2] A concerted effort by the United States to actualize these ideals began in earnest in the early 1960s.

The fundamental change in the nature of nuclear deterrence after October 1957, from American monopoly to superpower bipolarity, as a result of the Soviet Union's acquisition of an intercontinental nuclear projection capability, motivated the United States to promote vigorously integration as the most desirable basis for European security. While the Eisenhower administration had acknowledged the need for the Alliance to adapt its goals and strategy to the new situation, the emphasis on political and military integration received its first formal expression in a report on NATO's future, commissioned by President Kennedy in 1961. A study group chaired by former Secretary of State Dean Acheson wrote what eventually became National Security Action Memorandum (NSAM) 40, the guiding principles of the Kennedy administration's European security policy.

NSAM 40, one analyst observes, "seemed to rest implicitly on a view of the alliance as a cohesive unit in which tasks could be parcelled out by the United States."[3] The report of a delegation of the Western European Union (WEU)[4] visiting the United States in 1962 noted, "Remarks made by American political leaders indicated . . . that by 'partnership' the United States understands primarily a stronger initiative on the part

of the European NATO allies in the field of political consultation."[5]
Tighter integration and an agenda that went beyond article five of the
North Atlantic Treaty would ensure the American *droit de regard* over
European security, which the credibility of massive nuclear retaliation
had provided until then.

Furthermore, as the integration concept evolved, American statesmen
realized that it also served the purpose of stabilizing intra-Alliance
relations. Thomas Hughes, then Director of the Bureau of Intelligence
and Research at the State Department, pointed out to the secretary of
state in 1965 that "even if the Alliance did not serve Western defense
needs its members would still value it for intra-Western political
purposes."[6] American goals in emphasizing the need for integration
were, therefore, twofold: first, to preserve U.S. leadership in light
of a fundamental change in the prevailing security threat; second, to
encourage stability in intra-European relations.

In contrast to integration, cooperation emphasized total national
independence of decision-making, though not isolationism. Meeting
with Secretary of State Rusk in 1964, President Charles de Gaulle
explained, "It is not necessary to be integrated to be allied." He pointed
to French support for the United States in the Cuban Missile Crisis
as evidence of the ability of two or more nations to have a robust
mutual security relationship without formal, automatic commitment of
a prescribed level of forces.[7] The essence of this concept was further
spelled out in de Gaulle's letter to President Johnson communicating
France's withdrawal from NATO's integrated command in 1966. De
Gaulle wrote, "Unless in the three coming years events change the
basic facts directing East-West relations, [France] would, in 1969 and
beyond, be determined, as today, to fight on the side of its allies in the
event that one of them should be the object of unprovoked aggression."[8]
In other words, this was a pledge of continued adherence to article five
of the North Atlantic Treaty. But the distinctive feature of the pledge
was that France would decide when and how to join its allies, rather
than agree to a set of predetermined conditions as to troop placement,
command, and so forth.

As for the division of labor within Europe, de Gaulle foresaw
a cooperative regime led by a Franco-German entente rather than
by the United States. As one American analyst saw it, the various
autonomous states "would formulate common policies by unanimous
consent, independently of the United States, but under general French

leadership."[9] This implied transcending the mold of NATO's institutional framework, in which spirit France signed the Elysée Accord of 1963 with Germany. A year later de Gaulle tried to reach a similar agreement with Italy, only to be rebuffed by the Italian president's observation that NATO precluded the need for such an arrangement.[10] De Gaulle's annoyance at the futility of his attempt to piece together a parallel security framework supports John Duffield's observation that the French leader "seems to have been acutely aware of the tremendous power of institutional forces, which he sought to thwart at every turn."[11] However, the failure to ratify alternative terms of defense commitment did not imply Europe's rejection of the Gaullist philosophy.

Which concept Western Europe would accept, the American or the French, was ambiguous until 1967, and has actually remained so, albeit to a lesser extent, since then. While the United States tried to portray the Gaullist vision as extremist and the product of pride and obstinacy rather than rational, strategic thinking, certain tenets of Gaullism found widespread support in Europe. The European Alliance members had to weigh their faith in the American deterrent against the attractiveness of the French-led movement for the primacy of national independence in all security-related decisions.

THE DEBATE IN THE EARLY 1960s

The Alliance's consideration of an ideal balance between cooperation and integration offers an instructive frame of reference for the security watershed of the late Twentieth Century. While the political environment has changed drastically, the same generic issues that animated the 1960s, especially those concerning nuclear deterrence, are likely to reemerge in the 1990s.

In the early 1960s, as Europeans increasingly questioned the credibility of extended deterrence, their preferences tipped toward the French concept of security. In 1961, for instance, Europeans were very critical of the American call to improve conventional defense capabilities, as proposed in National Security Action Memorandum 40. They perceived this policy as a weakening of the nuclear guarantee. The general loss of favor for the American concept prompted the Kennedy administration gradually to back down from the original program of NSAM 40.[12]

The appointment of General Maxwell Taylor as Chairman of the U.S. Joint Chiefs of Staff in 1962 further confirmed European doubts. In his book *The Uncertain Trumpet*, Taylor had argued that "atomic war is indivisible" (i.e., a wall cannot separate theater from global nuclear exchanges) and that, therefore, the United States should use nuclear weapons only if American territory is attacked directly.[13] This indicated to Europeans that the United States would probably be extremely reluctant to initiate the use of nuclear weapons on Europe's behalf. (This is precisely the concern France's neighbors express today when French leaders insist that the *force de frappe*, nationally controlled, is *de facto* a European deterrent.) Such fears tipped the balance further toward the French concept of loose cooperation. If the American nuclear deterrent could not be relied on, then what did the Allies stand to gain by compromising their decision-making autonomy through integration? This question, which France had posed, gained greater attention over the course of the decade.

Exacerbating the fear that the United States might not be willing to use nuclear weapons in the defense of Europe was the inverse fear that the United States might jeopardize European security by launching nuclear weapons without European consent. American handling of the Cuban Missile Crisis gave substance to the latter concern. That experience highlighted a fundamental tenet of Gaullism: the vital interests of European states and the United States may be similar but are clearly not the same. Integration mixed with exclusive dependence on a nuclear force geographically removed from the European continent could, therefore, be suicidal for Europe. Thus, as one account of the Crisis concluded, "means correctly chosen for the greater problem [i.e., the Cuban Missile Crisis] have had a dampening effect upon the lesser one. And de Gaulle, in obvious ways, has been the beneficiary."[14]

Following on the heels of the Cuban Crisis, the Nassau Agreement between the United States and Great Britain, whereby the former would provide the latter with submarine-based Polaris missiles, compounded European anxieties even further and increased sympathy for France in Europe. Nassau emphasized the existence of a nuclear hierarchy within the Alliance, substantiating French criticism. The Federal Republic's Chancellor Adenauer stood by the injured party, and 1963 became the high water mark for the French vision of Alliance security.

Entering 1963, France benefitted from European doubts that had accrued over the past two years about American leadership, as well as from recently proven French nuclear weapons capability. France demonstrated its new position of influence forcefully with two major initiatives: rejection of British membership in the European Economic Community and signing the Treaty of Friendship and Cooperation with the FRG, a cooperative security arrangement outside of the NATO framework.

Within NATO de Gaulle made a concerted effort to block the American attempt to institutionalize force planning, as such integration ran counter to the French concept of security. France objected strongly to NATO proposal MC 100/1, which would have mandated increasing conventional forces in the Alliance in order to meet the force goals decided on at the 1952 Lisbon summit.

The debate between MC 100/1 and MC 14/2 (the existing doctrine)—between flexible response and massive retaliation—manifested the more fundamental tension between integration and cooperation. Pursuing the goals of MC 100/1 would require sophisticated planning coordination that only integration could provide, while sticking by MC 14/2 would be much less demanding on individual states, facilitating a simpler commitment to cooperation. As discussed in the introduction, force planning is a critical repository of leadership in a security regime. A loss of American influence in this area could have been extremely damaging. Thomas Finletter, then the U.S. permanent representative to NATO, appreciated the importance of the force planning debate and warned in 1963: "It can be assumed that when positions of Great Britain and FRG become generally known, France's position will appear a much less isolated position than might be inferred from voting on 100/1. Indeed, when positions become known, France's position is not likely to appear much more extreme on one end of spectrum than US's is on other. Indeed, there is danger involved in making this apparent."[15] The U.S. ultimately softened its insistence and postponed a new force planning doctrine until France withdrew from the integrated military structure in 1966.

Thus 1963 was marked by bolder assertion and broader acceptance of the French concept of cooperative security in Europe. Crippled force planning, Franco-German entente outside NATO, and increasing European concerns about the commitment of the United States to extended deterrence represented a shift of preferences in Europe toward a vision of looser cooperation. But the "victory" for France was only temporary.

THE MULTILATERAL NUCLEAR FORCE

The competition between the American and French visions of European security came to a head over the American proposal for a sea-based
multilateral nuclear force (MLF). Of the particular disputes that served
as surrogates for an open clash over general philosophical differences,
MLF had become the prominent channel by 1964. It was this issue
that highlighted the importance of garnering German support for one or
the other vision of the Alliance. Then, as now, because of its strategic
location and size of population, Germany's decision ultimately would
determine whether Europe would adopt a framework of integration or
of cooperation. Even if Germany could not initiate the terms of the
debate, its role was (and is) pivotal.

In October 1964, as a determination of the fate of the MLF approached, Walter Rostow, Chairman of the Policy Planning Council at
the State Department, alerted the secretary of state, "We are heading into
a major turning point, one way or the other, in the future of Europe and
of [the American] relation to Europe. . . . I cannot help observing that
the turning point of 1965 will be quite as important as that of 1947."[16]
According to Rostow, the fundamental basis of Alliance security as
conceived by the United States was concentrated in the MLF. France
attached similar importance to the issue. The American ambassador
to France, Charles Bohlen, wrote, also in October 1964, "De Gaulle
believes that the entire future of Germany as 'European,' rather than a
state tied to the U.S. orbit, as well as the future orientation of Europe are
at stake in this affair."[17] Connected with the ultimate fate of MLF, both
sides believed, would be a decisive commitment to one or the other extreme of a European security order—either integration or cooperation.

That perception, in 1964, of the stakes riding on MLF is significant
once again in the 1990s, as the French this time speak increasingly of a
"Europeanization" of deterrence. The major weakness of the MLF from
the European point of view was the American veto power over launch
control. A similar dilemma may be expected to emerge if France tries
to justify the continued deployment of the *force de frappe*, beyond the
Cold War, in a nominally European role. Although formal control of
the *force de frappe* is structurally different than the MLF would have
been, they are similar in that both would boast multinational protection
while ultimately remaining under the control of a single nation.

The dilemma of single-nation control over a multi-national deterrent crystallizes the tension between national sovereignty and alliance

commitment. Inevitably, the promise of one country to sacrifice its existence in order to preserve the vital interests of another country cannot be absolutely credible. The pledge that the United States would extend nuclear deterrence to Europe, even if backed by American soldiers stationed in Europe as "hostages"—a visible symbol of American commitment—requires a large degree of faith on the Europeans' part. By making this commitment, the United States compromises some of its sovereignty; however, were it not to make the commitment, the United States would violate its fundamental contribution to European security and would compromise credibility. The existence of this dilemma obviously raises doubts in Europe. Despite numerous promises and demonstrations of good faith, it is impossible for the United States to prove that in a crisis it would put Alliance commitment above sovereignty.

Under de Gaulle, (and since de Gaulle), France relied on the argument that the credibility gap inherent in the concept of American extended deterrence could be narrowed by basing European deterrence instead on a French nuclear force. The control of nuclear weapons by a nation on the European continent, according to this theory, should alleviate Europe's doubts about the American nuclear guarantee.[18]

Although national interests among European states were distinct, they faced the same physical risks, something the United States could not claim, even with troops in Europe. Europeans' vital interests, for which they would require the protection of nuclear weapons, were less dissimilar among themselves than between themselves and the United States. The logic which General Georges Fricaud-Chagnaud suggested in an essay written in 1986 was equally relevant twenty years earlier: "Deterrence or not, nothing will make the Rhine as wide as the Atlantic."[19] In essence, according to the French argument, because the European states are geographically contiguous, the control of nuclear weapons by a single one of those states would be virtually the same as control by them all and would be, therefore, a credible deterrent. No further political integration would be necessary. As a counter-argument the United States would have to propose a more attractive means for Western Europe to gain control over nuclear weapons. Hence, the multilateral nuclear force.

The MLF, however, had the drawback of an American veto privilege. To compete with the *force de frappe* for European approval, the MLF would have to hold out the promise of complete European control. An advisor to President Kennedy warned in early 1963 that refusal to consider a European nuclear force unconstrained by an American veto would "leave to General de Gaulle the chance to pose as the one true spokesman of real independence for Europeans." He observed that even Jean Monnet, the staunch critic of de Gaulle's aversion for tight European and trans-Atlantic integration, "underlined the requirement of nuclear autonomy for the new Europe."[20] In fact, West Germany insisted that an MLF agreement incorporate provisions for future Europeanization of control over the nuclear force. The United States' condition for relinquishing its intended privileged position of control was the political integration of participating states, such that they could act as a single unit.

Therefore, the decisions of non-nuclear European states to support either the *force de frappe* or the MLF would clearly indicate whether they accepted cooperation or integration in Alliance security. Choosing the *force de frappe* would demonstrate a state's belief that geographical integration was sufficient assurance that a nuclear force under one state's control, namely France, would be a credible deterrent for all states in Western Europe, and that Allies need only pledge to cooperate in a crisis, rather than establish a complex network of common peacetime planning. Opting for the MLF, on the other hand, would indicate a state's acceptance of the need for close political integration as a precondition for truly credible nuclear deterrence in Europe.

A critical dimension of this dichotomy was each side's labeling of its own position as fundamentally "Europeanist," and of the other side's as inherently divisive. MLF proponents argued that by holding out an incentive for political integration the force would encourage a solid European voice in security.

De Gaulle and other opponents of MLF, by contrast, observed that pursuit of such a concept, rather than strengthen Europe's collective voice, would instead unearth hazardous fault lines. One American analyst warned of "the possibility that the MLF, by deepening political divisions within the Alliance, would retard the movement toward European unity." Furthermore, he observed, if Europe were to integrate politically to the point where an MLF could become a European nuclear force, the MLF would, paradoxically, no longer be needed. "Such a force could be built on the nucleus of the British and French forces [instead]."[21]

De Gaulle's detractors, in turn, accused the French president of hypocritically twisting the meaning of integrationist terminology. A report on the European Parliament's stand on MLF noted, "The Gaullists are now warping the meaning of the touchstones of Europeanism for completely contrary goals. The 'Europeans' want to force de Gaulle to reveal his true colors on European matters."[22]

The underlying confusion stemmed from a misperception of what each side meant by European unity. To the United States and other MLF supporters, unity implied integration; when de Gaulle spoke of MLF as harmful to unity he appeared hypocritical from their point of view. To de Gaulle, unity implied cooperation amongst independent, sovereign states; he would have rejected assertions that MLF was consistent with this concept, particularly if control of the force rested in the last instance on an American veto.

De Gaulle's ambivalent policy guidance compounded the ambiguity of language. In almost all areas of foreign policy, the French president exercised decision-making exclusively, only rarely consulting his advisors, even Foreign Minister Maurice Couve de Murville. The one domain in which de Gaulle did allow Couve some policy-making latitude was anything that smacked of European supranationalism, as the president was very reluctant to take personal part in issues of that nature.[23] MLF was a gray area, at once an eminently national and supranational issue. De Gaulle provided policy guidance, but rather sporadically.

At first, stated policy was that France would not participate in an MLF, but neither would it stand in the way of others' participation. Then, in the autumn of 1964, French statesmen, including Ambassador to the United States Hervé Alphand and Couve, began to drop hints that the MLF would injure the possibility of European unity and would harm Franco-German relations. They insisted, however, that these were personal opinions and not official policy statements.[24] In November 1964, Couve did acknowledge to American Ambassador Charles Bohlen that French policy on MLF had, in fact, shifted to active opposition.[25]

Other European states echoed French ambivalence on MLF. Great Britain, Italy, Belgium and the Netherlands, in particular, had to balance the appeal of participation in MLF against the perceived risk of French retribution. In late 1964 they feared that France might link Europe's decision on MLF to grain price unification in the European Economic Community (EEC), the failure of which, they believed, would have destroyed the Common Market. They were also concerned about the consequences of supporting MLF only to find it abandoned a month later, and then being isolated in a French-led Europe. Finally, when it appeared that the United States and the FRG might proceed with

MLF bilaterally, the smaller countries adopted France's concerns about German rearmament. A major objective, from their point of view, was to co-opt Germany in a clear institutional framework. France appeared to present a viable, less risky alternative in the *force de frappe*.[26]

European indecision on MLF in the latter part of 1964 was very disconcerting to the United States. In a conversation with the French Permanent Representative to NATO, François Seydoux, in October 1964, Thomas Finletter pointed out that "it was very difficult for the U.S. to believe that none of its Allies [except] Germany would respond to American policy advocated by the U.S. at the highest level."[27] Thomas Hughes advised the secretary of state to proceed cautiously on MLF, noting that while continued perception in Europe of movement toward a bilateral German-American concept might induce the other states to decide, the United States might be dissatisfied with their decision.[28]

The United States had to weigh two imperatives at this juncture: the objective of pressing ahead with the MLF as a vehicle for the more basic American concept of European integration and the need to avoid a situation that would leave the United States clearly "defeated" vis-à-vis France. Hughes wrote, in October 1964, "The starkly integratory character of the MLF is out of context with the pace of developments in Europe. There is a general feeling that political evolution must spring gradually from dialogues among Europeans followed by slow steps ahead." As with conventional force planning, the United States opted for caution. From late 1964 the MLF died a slow death, which was finally pronounced toward the end of 1965.

This detailed illustration of how the integration-cooperation competition was played out through the MLF debate raises important questions for modern-day European security. As political tensions between East and West are relaxed, conventional forces in Europe are withdrawn, and major strategic nuclear weapons reductions are anticipated, the presence of a French nuclear force will become more conspicuous. Particularly if short-range nuclear weapons are removed from Germany, (as appears likely), the question must reemerge as to whether the *force de frappe* is credible as a European deterrent. If Western Europe accepts the French force as such, would this sound the death knell for the American concept of trans-Atlantic integration? Would primary European reliance on a French-controlled deterrent placate potential German aspirations for a nuclear capability? Could France move beyond rhetoric in establishing its nuclear force as a truly European nuclear force without compromising its national autonomy in security policy? Perhaps most important, if France could not credibly demonstrate the pan-European quality of its deterrent, would this impede the achievement of a French-led security order? The MLF debate never resolved these questions, because the MLF concept was withdrawn without Europe having to decide one way or the other between the United States and France. However, as this analysis has tried to demonstrate, it did highlight major dimensions of the integration-cooperation dichotomy in general and in the special case of nuclear weapons control. We will come back to those dimensions in chapters three and four when we look at the likely features of a future French-led European security order.

FRANCE'S WITHDRAWAL FROM NATO

Before turning to an analysis of the prospects for French leadership at lower conventional force levels, it is important to understand the impact of France's withdrawal from NATO's integrated military structure in 1966, the event which, in hindsight, appears to have been only a temporary resolution to the conflict between integration and cooperation.

France's announcement of its withdrawal from NATO's integrated military structure in March 1966 was the culmination of a buildup of conditions antithetical to the French concept of cooperation in European security. Disagreement with the other Allies over force planning procedures, strategy, operational concepts, and the proliferation of tactical nuclear weapons under dual control convinced de Gaulle to remove French forces and infrastructure from NATO command, with the understanding that France would continue to abide by its promise to cooperate with the Allies in defending against an unprovoked attack.

An immediate impact of de Gaulle's initiative was formal adoption by the Alliance of many of the institutional mechanisms which France had formerly blocked. In November 1966 NATO expanded the functions of the Defense Planning Committee (DPC), from which France opted out. Formerly responsible for force planning only, the DPC's agenda was now generalized to encompass any defense-related activities in which France was not a participant.[29]

A month later the Alliance approved a new force planning exercise, similar to the concept of MC 100/1 which France had obstructed. The main innovation of the new exercise was the requirement that political as well as military guidance inform future force planning. This concept was intended as a method of rationalization. By establishing a regular procedure for determining force contribution requirements for each member country, the exercise helped to ensure that commitments would be met.

Also in December, the newly empowered DPC created the Nuclear Defense Affairs Committee (NDAC) and the Nuclear Planning Group (NPG). The former would be an open forum for all Alliance members to participate in political consultation on nuclear matters. The latter would be the primary consultative body for nuclear decision-making, during crises as well as peacetime, and would consist of the United States, the Federal Republic of Germany, Great Britain, Italy, and three rotating members.

Each of these measures helped to build the tightly integrated regime which the United States had envisioned since the late 1950s. Underlying these new decision-making mechanisms were the two main pillars of the American concept of NATO: flexible response strategy and a broad agenda, encompassing political as well as military issues. Flexible response had first been proposed as official NATO strategy by U.S. Secretary of Defense McNamara at the Athens NATO ministerial meeting in May 1962. McNamara emphasized a renewed commitment to conventional options for the defense of the West, while retaining a range of nuclear options. The European, and especially the French, reaction at the time was fear that by this proposal the United States hoped to excuse itself from its commitment to massive nuclear retaliation in response to an attack on Western Europe, as called for by NATO strategy, according to MC 14/2. Sensitive to this reaction, particularly as France gained influence in Europe, the United States had to postpone discussion of flexible response.

During the course of the decade the United States negotiated arrangements with European Allies whereby tactical nuclear weapons were deployed on European soil and controlled under "dual key" systems, so that a decision to launch would require the approval of the nation on whose soil the weapons were based as well as American approval. This initiative helped to boost confidence that NATO might be able to respond to a Warsaw Pact attack through a variety of means and would not necessarily be forced to rely on intercontinental nuclear weapons. By the time of France's withdrawal, the other NATO members had become amenable to the idea of flexible response—as the doctrine had

transformed from a conventional- to a nuclear-heavy interpretation—
and adopted it as Alliance strategy in 1967.

The other pillar of the post-1966 European security regime was
encompassed in the Harmel Report of 1967. This document, drafted
by Belgian Foreign Minister Pierre Harmel, reaffirmed the concept
established in the North Atlantic Treaty that NATO should serve not
only a military role, but also a diplomatic role in political issues bearing
on the security interests of its members. In particular, NATO should
serve as the voice of the West in the process of détente. This idea became
the basis for the extension of NATO's agenda and the institutionalization
of new integrated policy-making mechanisms, mostly in the area of arms
control. Under this new mandate, for instance, the director of the U.S.
Arms Control and Disarmament Agency began to appear regularly
before the North Atlantic Council (NATO's main policy-making body)
from 1968, and the United States even led special Council meetings
to discuss the annual agenda of the General Assembly of the United
Nations.[30]

The proliferation of new processes for Alliance policy-making on a
wide variety of issues helped to firmly entrench American leadership
and consummated the transition to the broad agenda and tight integration
which has characterized NATO up to 1990. Lest France try to impede
this movement, as it did remain associated with NATO's political side,
the Harmel Report established that "no government was obliged to
associate itself with consultative efforts, but neither did it have the
right to prevent others from going ahead."[31] Thus, from all appearances,
by 1967 the United States had "won" the competition with France over
the future shape of security in Europe. However, beneath the surface,
the outcome was less clear cut.

First, flexible response hardly constituted a permanent solution to
differences within the Alliance over strategic needs. The doctrine is so
vague as to invite multiple interpretations. The mix of conventional and
nuclear force levels required to sustain flexible response is completely
subjective. As Jane Stromseth remarks, "In seeming to be all things
to all people, the compromise of flexible response allowed NATO to
mask—but not resolve—the clash of views in the Alliance over how far
NATO should rely on non-nuclear forces for deterrence and defence."[32]
This became vividly apparent in 1989, when the (then) FRG and the
United States disputed the fate of short-range nuclear forces in Europe.
As the United States saw it, these weapons were a crucial rung on the

ladder of escalation and a linchpin of flexible response and, therefore, inviolable. West Germany, increasingly hopeful for reunification, was less convinced of their necessity.

A Germany on the threshold of unification continued to press this logic in 1990. At the June NATO summit, Chancellor Kohl again expressed interest in eliminating both short-range missiles and nuclear artillery from Europe.

As Stromseth suggests, because the concept of flexible response is so ambiguous, its meaning at any given time is dependent on the particular force posture in being.[33] In other words, forces have tended to determine the meaning of doctrine, rather than the other way around. Secretary of Defense McNamara originally envisioned greater reliance on conventional weapons for the defense of Western Europe. However, by 1967 France's withdrawal and the increase in the number of tactical nuclear weapons deployed in Europe may have precluded that option. Europeans perceived the threat from the East as so immense that NATO's ability to counter it with conventional weapons was doubtful even if France were in the integrated military structure. Moreover, they believed, the growth in variety and quantity of nuclear weapons in Europe compensated for conventional deficiencies. Therefore, the meaning of flexible response in 1967 rested on the critical role of tactical nuclear weapons.

In the 1990s, the advent of extremely low force levels may return the Alliance to the original meaning of flexible response, as conceived by McNamara. The unprecedented reduction of the Soviet threat may convince NATO of the realistic possibility of relying primarily on conventional defense in the future. This will certainly be true as short- and long-range nuclear weapons are drawn down. A return to "true" flexible response is a likely outcome for the short term and, as will be discussed in the next chapter, will require careful consideration of France's role in conventional defense.

In the long run, low force levels are likely to challenge the core of flexible response itself, not simply its momentary meaning. Even if force posture has affected the interpretation of strategy in the past, force posture itself has changed only marginally over twenty years and has not even come close to seriously jeopardizing strategy. In that stable environment, flexible response was able to accommodate various interpretations, since no party would have to declare its particular interpretation. The prospect of cuts to 50 percent or more below NATO's

1989 force levels, however, will reveal the fault lines that have existed all along, because member states will have to proclaim exactly what they see as current strategic priorities for Europe. As it becomes clear that flexible response is not a permanent institution, the basic concept it supports—close intra-Alliance integration—must also be questioned.

Therefore, with hindsight it appears that the American "victory" over France in shaping European security was tenuous. The vagueness of flexible response permitted a great deal of latitude in the amount of change in the international structure it could withstand. Adaptability, however, was mistaken for permanence. The impetus of extremely low force levels in the future may dispel that illusion and revive the dimensions of the original debate within the Alliance. France could have a new opportunity to reassert its position.

Moreover, the French "loss" in 1966 was as ambiguous as the American "victory." True, the United States did take advantage of this watershed to launch a wide range of new institutions in the Alliance in order to ensure American leadership, and Secretary of State Rusk did affirm, in 1967, that "in general, the Alliance had adapted to France's withdrawal from integrated military activities more effectively and more efficiently than many believed possible."[34] But by the act of withdrawal France exerted an impact on the Alliance which was probably greater than any influence it could have exercised from within at the time.[35]

Analyst Carl Amme observed three important ways in which de Gaulle's initiative had lasting effects on the future shape of European security.[36] First, due to uncertainty as to the commitment of French conventional forces, "the American strategic concept of flexible response that calls for conventional defense with a high nuclear threshold would become impossible." Second, French withdrawal demonstrated vividly to the other Allies the difference between integration and cooperation. Formerly, the distinction was considered subtle, as exhibited in the MLF debate. By withdrawing, France became a permanent model for the rest of Europe of the "other" alternative. Finally, France's actions "emphasized the hazardous link between conventional conflict and nuclear war." One justification offered for withdrawal was the fear that, as part of an integrated unit, France could be dragged into a nuclear war against its will. By making this case, France raised the consciousness of its neighbors. Germany and the smaller states, Amme noted, became more profoundly concerned about diverse nuclear dilemmas as a result.

Therefore, although the competition seemed over by 1967, the "loser" had left a strong legacy and the "winner" had established a dubious victory. The implications of that outcome were even more apparent in 1990 than they were 23 years earlier. At the time, the newly erected foundations of European security seemed permanent. Today it is becoming clear that the tension between integration and cooperation in the Alliance was only papered over. Drastically lower conventional force levels promise to reopen the controversy.

NOTES

1. For discussion of the two opposing visions, see, for example, Henry A. Kissinger, *The Troubled Partnership: A Re-Appraisal of the Atlantic Alliance* (Garden City, NY, Doubleday & Co., 1966), p. 49.

2. U.S. Department of State, *American Foreign Policy, 1950–1955, Vol. I* (Washington, DC, Government Printing Office, 1957), "The North Atlantic Treaty," 4 April 1949, pp. 812–15.

3. Jane E. Stromseth, *The Origins of Flexible Response* (London, The MacMillan Press, 1988), p. 35.

4. The Western European Union is the organization formed by the 1954 modification of the Brussels Treaty of 1948. The original Treaty included Belgium, France, Luxembourg, the Netherlands and the United Kingdom in a defense pact against a potentially resurgent Germany. Following France's rejection of a European Defense Community in 1954, the Federal Republic of Germany and Italy were allowed to accede to the Treaty. A council of Western European Union was created with vague competence for overseeing regional security. The organization has been perceived variously as the European pillar of NATO or as parallel and complementary to NATO.

5. "Washington against a 'Third Force,' " U.S. Department of State translation of article in *Frankfurter Allgemeine* (28 July 1962). Found in National Security Archive, Nuclear History Collection. NB: All historical documents used in this study are available at the National Security Archive, 1755 Massachusetts Ave., NW, Suite 500, Washington, DC 20036. This will be indicated henceforth as "NSA."

6. Cited in Stromseth, p. 106.

7. U.S. Embassy, Paris, *Meeting between de Gaulle and Rusk on MLF*, Telegram to U.S. Department of State (14 December 1964). NSA.

8. U.S. Department of State, *NATO Political Consultations: The Harmel Exercise; French Withdrawal and NATO Counter–Measures; The Troop Problem and Burdensharing; U.S. Relations with NATO*, Administrative History (circa January 1969). NSA.

9. D. E. Mark, *Considerations involving Germany and France which*

Are Pertinent to Modifications of the U.S. Position on MLF, White House Memorandum (4 November 1964). NSA.

10. Richard Helms, Deputy Director for Plans, Central Intelligence Agency, *Views of President Charles de Gaulle regarding the United States, Europe and NATO; and Italian Reaction*, Memorandum to Director of Central Intelligence (18 March 1964). NSA.

11. John Stuart Duffield, "The Evolution of NATO's Conventional Force Posture" (Ph.D. Dissertation, Princeton University, 1989), pp. 423–24.

12. Duffield, p. 340.

13. Cited in "Washington Against a 'Third Force' " (see this chapter, note 5). NSA.

14. *The U.S. and de Gaulle—The Past and the Future*, Memorandum to the President (30 January 1963), p. 4. [Author not indicated.] NSA.

15. Thomas K. Finletter, U.S. Embassy, Paris, *NATO Force Planning*, Telegram (POLTO 713) to Secretary of State (26 November 1963). NSA.

16. W. W. Rostow, *The Coming Crunch in European Policy*, Memorandum to the Secretary of State (12 October 1964). NSA.

17. Charles Bohlen, U.S. Embassy, Paris, *De Gaulle's Position on MLF*, Telegram to U.S. Department of State (31 October 1964). NSA.

18. This argument was advanced, for instance, at a meeting between Secretary of State Rusk and French Ambassador to the U.S. Hervé Alphand in November 1964, during which the latter's defense of the French independent *force de frappe* "seemed to rest on the fact that it was French controlled and hence wholly European in nature." Cited in D. H. McKillop (drafter), U.S. Department of State, *Meeting between Secretary of State Rusk and French Ambassador Alphand*, Telegram (924) to U.S. Embassy, Paris (15 November 1964). NSA.

19. Georges Fricaud–Chagnaud, "French Nuclear Deterrence and European Solidarity," in Robbin F. Laird, ed., *French Security Policy from Independence to Interdependence* (Boulder, CO, Westview Press, 1986), p. 125.

20. *The U.S. and de Gaulle—The Past and the Future* (see this chapter, note 14). NSA.

21. John Newhouse, *Balancing the Risks in the MLF Report* (20 March 1964), p. 10. NSA. Newhouse was a staff consultant on the U.S. Senate Foreign Relations Committee at the time.

22. U.S. Mission to the European Communities, Brussels, *European Parliament Views on MLF*, Airgram (ECBUS A 399) to U.S. Embassies in Europe (2 December 1964), p. 2. NSA.

23. Samy Cohen, *La Monarchie nucléaire* (Paris, Hachette, 1986), p. 89.

24. D. H. McKillop (drafter), U.S. Department of State, *Conversation between Ambassador Alphand and Secretary of State*, Telegram (733) to U.S. Embassy, Paris (23 October 1964). NSA.

25. Charles Bohlen, U.S. Embassy, Paris, *Meeting with Couve de Murville on MLF*, Telegram to Secretary of State (19 November 1964). NSA.

26. Memorandum of Conversation with Gerard Wissels, Chef de Cabinet Lindhorst Homan, and High Authority Thomas Fina, USEC, in U.S. Mission to the European Communities, *European Parliament Views on MLF* (see this chapter, note 22). Representative of European fears of upsetting France was the observation by Robert van Schendel, Secretary–General of the European Movement, that "whatever the inherent cohesive force of European economic integration, he doubted that it could resist the centrifugal thrust of division caused by the split between France and its NATO allies on defense matters." Memorandum of conversation with Robert van Schendel; Thomas Fina, USEC (24 November 1964), in U.S. Mission to the European Communities, *European Parliament Views on MLF*.

27. Thomas Finletter, *Conversation with French Permanent Representative to NATO, Seydoux*, Telegram (POLTO 595) to Secretary of State (19 October 1964). NSA.

28. Thomas L. Hughes, U.S. Department of State, Office of Intelligence and Research, *Western European and Soviet Reactions to the Idea of a U.S.–German Bilateral MLF Agreement*, Intelligence note to Secretary of State (7 October 1964). NSA.

29. Stromseth, p. 110.

30. U.S. Department of State, *NATO Political Consultations* (see this chapter, note 8).

31. U.S. Department of State, *NATO Political Consultations*.

32. Stromseth, p. 194.

33. Stromseth, p. 225. Duffield notes too that when MC 14/3 (flexible response doctrine) was first adopted, it could actually have been interpreted as allowing for conventional force reductions, and in some cases it did, in fact, lead to such change (Duffield, p. 415).

34. Secretary of State Dean Rusk, U.S. Congress, Senate, Combined Subcommittee of Foreign Relations and Armed Services Committees on the Subject of United States Troops in Europe, *United States Troops in Europe*, Hearing before the Combined Subcommittee of Foreign Relations and Armed Services Committees on the Subject of United States Troops in Europe, 90th Cong., 1st Sess., 3 May 1967, pp. 60–61.

35. David Yost suggests, "France's nonbelligerency option may represent a difference in degree and candor rather than one of category. Indeed, France may actually be less likely to pursue nonbelligerency than some other Allies, depending on the circumstances." See David S. Yost, *France and Conventional Defense in Central Europe* (Boulder, CO, Westview Press, 1985), p. 110.

36. Carl H. Amme, Jr., *NATO without France: A Strategic Appraisal* (Stanford, Stanford University Press, 1967), pp. 158–59.

CHAPTER 2

FRENCH MILITARY POTENTIAL AT LOW FORCE LEVELS

Unlike the newly uniting Germany, France cannot hope to bring an exceptionally large population or a dominant economy to bear on the new Europe. The present opportunity for France to forge a new leadership role in Europe lies in the area of security and stems primarily from the leverage associated with its conventional and nuclear military assets. The value of this trump card (*atout*), as the French commonly refer to their armed forces, will increase as the United States withdraws forces from Europe and as further withdrawals appear imminent. Proportionately, the sheer bulk of French troops will comprise a larger percentage of residual forces on the European continent. As the most technically advanced of the European forces, the ability of the First Army, the *force d'action rapide* (FAR), and the Tactical Air Force (FATAC) to respond quickly to crises will become more critical. These initial observations should make intuitive sense, and they will be discussed more thoroughly below. Also, French commitment to provide territorial depth and to support logistically the return of American forces to Europe will become more important as the dynamics of a potential future battle increasingly favor mobility and as American commitment to Europe relies more on reinforcements rather than on forward–deployed troops.

A fundamental assumption of this analysis is that increasing relative military potential, such as France boasts today, will translate into political leverage in influencing the future of European security. French leaders' assessments of the current situation reflect this conviction. They emphasize the dangers and instabilities that must continue to be accounted for, frequently warning of the "strategic void" that threatens to evolve in the center of Europe. Former Defense Minister Jean–Pierre Chevènement has spoken of France's military capability, faced with this void, as "the guarantee of a durable peace on [the European] continent."[1] The chairman of the Senate Foreign Affairs and Defense Committee explains that the conjunction of continued instability and reduction, nevertheless, of western (especially American) armed forces "underlines the important and increased role that France must play in West European security."[2] On this basic point agreement spans the political spectrum in France—the Socialist Chevènement and the Gaullist former prime minister Jacques Chirac see eye to eye on this assertion, if not on its implications for policy. Indeed, the link between military capability and political leverage, supported by centuries of historical evidence, is not particularly astounding and normally would not require formal proof. One need only look at American diplomatic influence in the aftermath of the Persian Gulf war. However, the current revolution in the international political environment and the apparent return to a concert of Europe, as ideological lines rapidly dissolve, warrant a brief digression to justify the assertion that military power still confers a large degree of political clout in Europe.

While the idea of a Soviet–led attack on Western Europe seems more absurd with each passing day, the cold war mentality that evolved over forty years cannot be expected to fade overnight. It should not be surprising that western defense planners, accustomed to thinking in terms of a clear threat from the East, will probably remain skeptical for the foreseeable future. The term "reversibility" has been bandied about on both sides of the Atlantic, alluding to a possible upset of liberalism in Moscow. Tiananmen Square has become the favorite idiom for statesmen pointing to the danger of a reversal in the policies of apparently liberalizing communist regimes. Chevènement warns that, regardless of political context, the Soviet Union "will remain, *de facto*, the greatest military power on the continent at the beginning of the next century" and that "it will continue to weigh, as it has always done since the Eighteenth Century, on the European balance."[3] Concern that Soviet (or Russian) power could indeed be harnessed for aggressive aims was echoed by deputies of all parties in discussing the 1990 French defense budget.[4]

Similar arguments have also been put forward in the United States. The perception that the Soviet Union might continue to pose a threat to the West and that traditional elements within the Soviet leadership might gain power and exploit a still strong military machine for aggressive ends gained credibility, for example, with Moscow's use of force in the Baltic republics and Eduard Shevardnadze's resignation from the post of foreign minister, warning of dictatorship to come. Hence, doubts raised in early 1991 about whether the United States should ratify the Convential Forces in Europe (CFE) arms reduction treaty of November 1990.

Furthermore, as forty years of Cold War have demonstrated, threat perception is self–perpetuating, such that arguing on the basis of a "reversal" threat in order to justify immediate aims, such as passing a defense budget, will serve to embed that idea more firmly. Even if Soviet aggression may appear virtually to have disappeared from an objective point of view, more important to decision–making is the perception amongst political leaders, both in the United States and in Europe, that a complete turnaround is even remotely possible. As long as such a perception persists, military power will remain a key source of diplomatic influence. And the withdrawal of American forces from Europe, despite this perception, will elevate the importance of European military assets, foremost amongst them the French.

Even absent the Soviet threat or the perception of such a threat, it might be argued that military power would continue to confer political leverage. Perhaps more frightening today than any particular security threat is the less focused danger of sudden eruption in an unstable, multipolar political environment.

For forty years western publics have been conditioned to associate military preparation with the goal of countering an eventual Soviet–led attack from the East. Naturally, these publics looked for peace dividends and devalued the advantages inherent in a strong defense as they saw that threat dissipate. From the end of 1989, as democracy swept over Eastern Europe, military power seemed to slip behind economic power as the main source of diplomatic influence. For states that have a comparative advantage in military capability, first the United States, but also France and Great Britain, it was difficult to prove to their publics that the need for a strong defense effort transcends any single, visible enemy.

However, the events of early 1991 have reminded the West of post–cold war threats to security that may arise suddenly. Violent unrest in the Baltics and other republics of the Soviet Union and discord among the Yugoslav republics have undoubtedly opened many eyes, and the most effective lesson in the need for defense beyond the Cold War has been the Iraq crisis.

The war with Iraq and its successful outcome for the allied coalition put the value of military capability into a new light. One effect of the war may have been to break the conditioned link between defensive preparation and the Soviet threat. The crisis initiated the post–cold war world to new security risks. A lesson to all the countries of the world from which the United States and France will probably benefit diplomatically is the importance of sustaining robust military capability in order to reassure against rapidly arising, as opposed to more long–term and visible, threats.

If the very intangibility (relative to the cold war Soviet threat) of elements that might topple the prevailing condition of peace is the source of current anxieties, then the existence of stable, non–aggressive military safeguards to hedge against such uncertainty should be highly valued. Within Europe, France is an ideal guarantor in this regard, lacking the cold war stigma of superpower status, while possessing a strong, highly mobile military capability and encouraging an orderly transition in Europe. The critical nature of this role is a function both of the political environment and of the prospect of extremely low force levels.

In a 1985 study, analyst David Yost determined, "Current and planned French conventional forces would probably not decisively affect an East–West conflict in Europe *unless the Warsaw Pact withheld a great deal of its conventional combat power*" (my emphasis).[5] Conversely, as the Pact dissolves and the Soviet Union withdraws military forces, according to the CFE Treaty of November 1990, future multilateral agreements, and unilateral decisions, a threshold will be approached at which the marginal value of early, active French participation in Western European defense during a crisis would become critical. This overview will not try to define that threshold, but it will describe the dynamics by which the threshold is approached. The concept of extremely low force levels is here understood to mean reductions of hardware by 50 percent or more of 1989 NATO levels in the Atlantic–to–the–Urals (ATTU) region.[6]

FRANCE'S WITHDRAWAL FROM NATO:
THE MILITARY IMPACT

Until the events of 1989, the significance of France's conventional contribution to European security was dubious. The debate, prompted by French withdrawal from the integrated military structure in 1966, over how dependent NATO would be on the availability of French ports, railroads, air bases, communications, etcetera during a crisis as well as the impact of non–participation of French troops in forward defense prov ed relatively inconclusive. The immediate reaction of leading American political leaders at the time was mixed.

Testifying before Congress in 1967, Secretary of Defense Robert McNamara dismissed the impact of the French initiative, adding that "the rail and road communication net in the low countries is a far more efficient one and a far more responsive one than the rail and road conditions that we would be depending on in France." Actual benefits accruing from the change, according to McNamara, included American foreign exchange savings and a needed push for scaling down staff sizes.[7] Similarly, Congressman Chet Holifield, Chairman of the Joint Committee on Atomic Energy (a committee that, traditionally, did not look kindly on French security policy), observed that "neither the military strength nor the geography of France is vital to a strong Alliance between the United States and the other free nations of Western Europe."[8]

Furthermore, French withdrawal was not the first shock to NATO military planning. The initiative echoed changes in the British commitment to the Alliance in 1957, when "complete disintegration of Britain's forces as to leave the vital North German plain virtually defenseless" gave a new impetus, according to American military leaders, to the need to deploy intermediate–range ballistic missiles in NATO Europe.[9] Indeed, the transition to increased reliance on tactical nuclear weapons rather than conventional armament over the course of the 1960s probably damped the effect of de Gaulle's decision.

As analyst Brigadier Kenneth Hunt observed, the commitment of French military forces to NATO may always have been doubtful. In time of crisis, the Supreme Allied Commander Europe (SACEUR) would have to request troops from France, as from any other ally, and given the philosophical tension, it was never certain when France would comply (i.e., before or after hostilities had begun). The withdrawal in 1966 may have simply made this fact explicit.[10] Furthermore, even if France could be expected to fight beside its Allies during a war (regardless of how it might respond to a pre–war crisis), its military capability had decreased significantly since the end of the war in Algeria in 1961. From an immediate post–Algeria total of 1,023,000 officers and troops in January 1962, France had reduced its strength by 43 percent to 581,000 by January 1967.[11] From this perspective, then, French actions had already precluded building a credible conventional defense in the Alliance, and the act of withdrawal was little more than a formality.

Yet, while Hunt and Amme judged the military impact of French departure to have been relatively muted when measured against expectations and the actual political impact, they did acknowledge several substantive strategic implications which may have crippled NATO considerably. Although France had drawn down its ground forces since Algeria, its 450–plane air force remained relatively formidable. "The conventional and reconnaissance capability of the French Air Force," according to Hunt, "was a loss less easily made good."[12] Of the land forces that France did retain, the 65,000 troops of the Second Corps remained stationed at Baden, in the western part of the FRG, but obviously could not be considered as automatically useable by SACEUR, and, therefore, might have been seen as a hindrance, occupying valuable space that could have been used to station troops integrated in NATO.[13] Even more disruptive were necessary modifications of logistics.

Four basic logistical dilemmas resulted from France's withdrawal. First, not being able to count on the availability of French territory reduced the effective operational depth of NATO's central region, for planning purposes, to about 200 km from the inter–German border to the French border at their closest points and about 400 km at their farthest. (The terrain is, coincidentally, least mountainous, and therefore least defensible, where the depth is narrowest.) Perceptually this was very important, as it constrained assumptions about NATO's ability to trade space for time during a battle. In other words, knowing that the distance through which Allied forces would be able to withdraw, while still maintaining a credible defense, was considerably reduced would affect decisions about how to counter an attack, which would, in turn, seriously influence the outcome of battle (i.e., NATO might accept more attrition before withdrawing than it would if it knew it could rely on the availability of French territory.) On this subject, Senator Stuart Symington remarked with some alarm in 1967, "When we had the

[Berlin] airlift, you could hardly take off from Frankfurt before you were over East Germany." He recalled, further, General Arthur Gruenther having told him in 1954 that for this very reason it would be "absolutely impossible" to have a "meaningful NATO without France."[14]

Corollary to modification of withdrawal assumptions, as Amme observed, was the inability of NATO to adopt a defense in depth from the Rhine and Weser Rivers.[15] (This is an issue which is gaining relevance in the 1990s, as massive force reductions are foreseen.) The logic behind a defense in depth is that it allows the defender time to determine the focus of an enemy attack and to position forces optimally. By establishing the forward line of troops further west from the inter–German border, NATO forces would increase the window of time in which they might observe and react in preparing to fend off an attack from the East. However, France's withdrawal constrained the ability to trade space for time, so the option of defense in depth was also precluded. (In fact, the issue was mostly academic anyway, because for political reasons the FRG would not accept a defense in depth, which would imply a NATO willingness to give away German territory. However, in a unified Germany, with troops stationed in the western portion only, a defense in depth will, essentially, have been established.)

Additionally, the reduction of operational depth required NATO to concentrate command and control assets in a smaller area. While closer proximity enhanced coordination among these nodes, safety through dispersal was lost. The transfer of major headquarters from Paris to sites in Belgium, the Netherlands, and the FRG facilitated simplification of command, but as a result, "three major headquarters were within 100 miles of each other, in a crowded part of Europe," and were, therefore, more vulnerable.[16]

The second logistical dilemma that became apparent in 1966 concerned the security of lines of communication (LOCs) for the resupply and reinforcement of NATO during a crisis or war. Not only was NATO no longer able to plan on the assured availability of French ports, railroads and highways, but the LOCs that were to replace routes through France as the main axes of reinforcement now ran parallel to the inter–German border—North to South from Belgium, the Netherlands and northern Germany, rather than East to West— and were, therefore, more susceptible to being cut off at any point by Warsaw Pact air interdiction. "In some cases," Amme noted, "the lines of communication are closer to the border than the casernes of the troops being supplied."[17] One high–ranking American officer, formerly serving at Supreme Headquarters Allied Powers Europe (SHAPE), confirmed that of the strategic ramifications of France's withdrawal in 1966, this was perhaps the most disturbing.[18]

Related to access to LOCs was the third logistical dilemma, which concerned France's geographical position as a "land and air bridge" connecting NATO's central region with its southern flank. Without the availability of French territory and air space, the two sectors would effectively be cut off from each other by a barrier of neutral countries. Hunt argued that "if transit or overflying and landing rights are denied, the loss would be a serious one." This would be particularly true during a period of crisis leading to war.[19] The use of French air space for Allied operations in approximately 100,000 flights per year, prior to France's withdrawal, demonstrated NATO's dependence on France as a bridge to the central region.[20]

The final logistical dilemma prompted by French departure from the integrated military structure concerned the ability to disperse tactical air forces in a crisis. The Berlin Crisis of 1961 demonstrated the value a SACEUR would attach to the availability of French infrastructure for the deployment of air forces as tension mounted before a war (since this is when French status would be in question). Nine NATO air squadrons had been removed from French bases in 1959 in response to French refusal to stockpile NATO nuclear munitions on French soil. However, fearing the vulnerability of an "overconcentration of planes" on German and British bases at the time of the Crisis, then SACEUR Lauris Norstad recommended flushing NATO squadrons back to bases in France, with emergency arrangements negotiated for the temporary storage of nuclear ordnance.[21] Even if six bases would be sufficient for supporting the U.S. Air Force in Europe, Amme argued, basic tactical principles demand the option of "shifting frequently" aircraft to different active bases.[22]

Thus, in 1966 and 1967 arguments were made both asserting and denying the significance for the future of European security of France's withdrawal from NATO's integrated military structure. While Secretary McNamara and Congressman Holifield, amongst others, dismissed the impact and expressed their confidence in the Alliance's ability to adapt quickly, more skeptical observers, like Amme, suggested that de Gaulle's decision would "have a serious effect on the operation of the American strategic concept of flexible response in the case of any sizeable penetration."[23]

A key point in the latter assessment was the link between the French initiative and a particular strategic concept—flexible response. Only with a particular strategic framework in mind is it possible to determine whether France's withdrawal did or did not have a critical military impact. For instance, if NATO had continued to rely on massive retaliation in 1966, the effect would have been minimal. If, on the other hand, NATO had accepted flexible response completely and was intent on devoting the conventional resources to European defense which McNamara had encouraged, then the effect would have been truly crippling. As Hunt argued, "If NATO strategy was based on a full flexible response rather than primarily on deterrence, if there was unqualified acceptance that the full thirty divisions, for many years the goal, were essential for the defence in the Centre, the loss of the French troops would clearly have to be regarded as serious—and the French bargaining strength would be that much greater. But that is not the case."[24]

Hunt's point aptly summarizes the one definitive conclusion that can be drawn from the debate on the strategic import of France's withdrawal. Ultimately the answer depended on how much or how little NATO had accepted full flexible response. By 1966 it was clear that the proliferation of tactical nuclear weapons in NATO had encouraged an interpretation of this very ambiguous, compromise doctrine in favor of primary reliance on those weapons rather than on conventional defense. Therefore, despite its dramatic political effect, the French withdrawal probably had a minimal military effect, given the prevailing assumptions about how European security should be maintained.

Today, however, the advent of asymmetrical reductions of Soviet and East European conventional forces, the prospect of future parity at extremely low force levels, and the internal disintegration of the Warsaw Pact may set the stage for a return to (introduction of?) full flexible response. Increased confidence in the ability to defend Western Europe conventionally, coupled with a growing aversion to nuclear weapons, especially in Germany, may constitute the necessary conditions for the achievement of flexible response as McNamara intended, at the very moment, ironically, when NATO's future seems questionable. It is in this context that we will examine France's current military potential. If Western Europe is in practice returning to flexible response, then the significance of French participation should be relatively strong. This, it will be argued, is indeed the case.

FRANCE'S MILITARY CAPABILITY IN THE 1990s:
THE BEAN COUNT

At a first cut, it is important to recognize the simple mass of force that France would be able to contribute to European defense—the "bean count." According to the International Institute for Strategic Studies' *The Military Balance, 1990–1991*, French ground and air force manpower totals 371,000. NATO manpower in the central region of Europe (i.e., Belgium, the Netherlands, Luxembourg, Denmark and the western part of Germany) totals 1,016,700 (including the French II Corps in Baden, Germany). When the territory of France is added to this region, total manpower is 1,335,000, of which the French portion is 28 percent.[25] Given this mass, argued former West German Chancellor Helmut Schmidt in 1987, "French and German conventional forces alone would be almost enough to provide a counterweight to the massed conventional forces of the Soviet Union and to strike a balance of power."[26]

Imminent American troop withdrawals from Europe and unilateral or CFE–negotiated reductions by smaller Allies, seeking to gain their slice of the peace dividend, promise to magnify the weight of France's military presence in Europe. The United States and the Soviet Union have tentatively agreed to troop reductions to 195,000 each in Europe's central region. As a precondition for Soviet approval of unification, Germany has pledged to limit its army to 370,000 personnel, of which no more than 345,000 will be ground or air forces.[27] Great Britain plans to pull half of its 67,200 troops from Germany by the mid–1990s.[28] Meanwhile, French leaders repeat that France's land army will not fall below a complement of 250,000.[29]

Policy–making stability as well as demographic stability in France support this trend. For the French, military service is a major element behind the "national spirit of defense." Legislators and statesmen are very sensitive to any debate between the alternatives of conscription and *armée de métier* (professional army). In his address to the nation following the Gulf war, President Mitterrand emphasized that national protection and contribution to Europe's defense require "the participation of all citizens."[30] France is likely to maintain a fairly constant level of military manpower due, in part, to the assumed link between service and national culture. The other key factor which will keep this level stable is the relatively small projected population decline in France as compared with the rest of Western Europe.

France is not expected to be hit especially hard by the general demographic downturn predicted for Europe between 1990 and 2000. According to one estimate, France's population in 2025 will remain 55 million, the same level measured in 1985.[31] The number of men reaching age 18 (i.e., conscription age) in France will fall by only 9 percent between 1989 and 2000 (the smallest percentage decrease in Europe, along with Greece). In fact, in 1996 France will surpass Italy as the European nation with the highest population of men reaching 18 (with the exception of Turkey).[32] From this simple head–counting point of view, French manpower inputs should increase the relative weight of France's military presence in Europe as other countries' troops diminish. "Given American reluctance and a growing shortage of personnel in the Bundeswehr," remarks Pierre Lellouche, foreign policy advisor to former Prime Minister Jacques Chirac, "the contribution that conventional French forces would make as soon as a crisis broke is regarded as crucial."[33] The shift in relative strengths will, in turn, enhance French influence in shaping European security.

Furthermore, France possesses comparatively high quantities of weapons systems likely to become more important in the new defense environment. Most notable in this respect are its combat helicopters, light armored vehicles, and tactical air forces. These will all play a central role, since lower force levels will place a high premium on mobility.

In combat helicopters assigned primarily to close air support and air attack, France currently owns approximately 25 percent of the NATO total in the Atlantic–to–the–Urals region, according to official declarations made at the signing of the CFE Treaty in November 1990. This is the largest attack helicopter force held by any single party to the accord, with the exception of the U.S.S.R. Under the Treaty, NATO will be allowed to increase its holdings of attack helicopters to 2000, although it will not necessarily do so. France will cut its force to 352, which will constitute at least 18 percent of the NATO total.[34]

France's non–tank armored vehicles (i.e., armored personnel carriers, infantry fighting vehicles, and heavy armored fighting vehicles) account for 12 percent of the NATO total in the ATTU and 16 percent in the area of the central region and France.[35]

Finally, according to officially declared figures, France possesses 700 combat aircraft. Depending on which planes are counted, as some are nominally dedicated to air defense, while others are assigned to the tactical nuclear (prestrategic) mission, the French air force constitutes between 8 and 12 percent of NATO air power in the ATTU.[36] Both France and NATO as a whole are allowed under the CFE Treaty to increase combat aircraft holdings. Depending on how France and other parties act on this allowance, French air power could grow in relative importance in the future.

This rough sketch conveyed by bean counting illustrates that France has a significant contribution to bring to bear in European defense. That contribution is strong in the key dimension of mobility and will grow in importance as other countries (primarily the United States) withdraw forces from the continent. Placing the French force in a dynamic combat context supports this initial impression.

As a first step toward a more dynamic analysis, the value of French military power must be measured on a standard scale. One scale commonly used to measure military strength of land forces in Europe is the U.S. Army's Weapons Effectiveness Index/Weighted Unit Value (WEI/WUV) scale. The WEI/WUV method assigns effectiveness (WEI) points on a scale of zero to one to particular models within a given class of military hardware (i.e., tanks, armored personnel carriers, small arms, etc.), according to relative performance within that class. The number of units of that type of tank, armored personnel carrier (APC), artillery piece, etcetera is multiplied by the effectiveness points to get a WEI score. The class of hardware as a whole is then given a class weight, on a scale of zero to one hundred, according to determinations about its relative value in combat. The WEI score is multiplied by the class weight to get a WUV score. This is done for each class of military hardware in a country's arsenal (ground forces only), and the WUV scores are summed to attain an aggregate WUV score. By definition, every 99,314 WUV points constitute one armored division equivalent (ADE).

By this accounting, at full mobilization France's First Army and *force d'action rapide* plus reserves constitute about 4.47 ADEs, which represents approximately 13 percent of NATO's capability after twenty days of mobilization, (pre–CFE reduction). At full NATO mobilization, given the balance in 1991, the French contribution would be approximately 9.5 percent.[37] If the full force of France's military capability were deployed in NATO's Northern Army Group (NORTH-AG), as it might plausibly be, then within that particular region it would constitute an even larger proportion of the total.

While this contribution does seem considerable, the WEI/WUV model in fact hides certain strengths of the French force. WEI/WUV tends to highlight firepower and heaviness. Therefore, an army possessing a large number of main battle tanks receives high scores. However, a credible defense cannot be built on main battle tanks alone. In fact, massive force reductions will probably favor lightness and maneuverability, qualities in which the French military excels.

FRANCE'S MILITARY CAPABILITY IN THE 1990s: A MORE DYNAMIC ASSESSMENT

Extremely low force levels will induce a critical transformation in the type of scenario that might be envisioned for a future war in Europe. The buildup of elaborate conventional forces on both sides of the inter–German border over the past forty years meant that if war were to break out it would probably proceed according to an attrition–withdrawal dynamic. In other words, the Warsaw Pact would prosecute an attack across the border with a certain degree of aggressiveness, yielding a certain level of attrition in the West, according to which NATO would either hold its line or withdraw in order to recoup and gain time for reinforcement. Meanwhile, both alliances' air forces would support the ground battle by launching strikes against the other side's engaged forces and follow–on echelons. The Pact would modify its rate of prosecution according to the amount of attrition it suffered from day to day. The battle would continue in this fashion, with withdrawal and rate of attack prosecution acting as mechanisms for defender and attacker to achieve their respective goals, until one side suffered an unacceptable amount of attrition or until the defender withdrew an unacceptable distance. At that point a stalemate would be achieved (assuming nuclear weapons were withheld). At a very basic level of abstraction, that is the type of combat on which analysts of late twentieth century European security traditionally have based their arguments. It is, for instance, the nature of force–on–force interaction simulated in Joshua Epstein's Adaptive Dynamic Model.[38] At extremely low force levels, however, attrition and withdrawal may be complicated by more rapid maneuvering at key points.

A RAND study on the implications of low force levels in Central Europe determined that in combat in such an environment "rapid initial penetrations on main sectors are very likely."[39] Smaller forces might, for instance, be more adept at carrying out flanking operations—

rapidly driving through NATO defense at the flanks of corps sectors and disrupting reinforcements and communications in the rear. Also, as lighter units would be able to move quickly along a front, the focus of aggression might shift more often at lower force levels. These new circumstances might not be easily illustrated by existing models, but they are the very circumstances in which France's particular strengths would come into play. The strong possibility that future combat would emphasize tactical maneuver suggests a context conducive to more revealing analysis.

Over the past decade France has made important strides in operational concepts, force structure, and equipment, which indicate preparation for maneuver–type combat. A security expert from the French Ministry of Foreign Affairs, Benoit d'Aboville, observes, "We [France] have always been more influenced by mobility, the concept, than the NATO military [strategists], because we are in the rear; we have to move up very quickly, and we have to choose our movement line."[40] Choosing a position and moving quickly are critical elements of what Epstein calls "dexterity." This he defines as "the ability to *detect* evolving concentrations, *decide* what countering units are needed and where they should come from, *communicate* (securely) those decisions in the form of orders to the chosen units, and *move* those units to the threatened area, all of this before it is too late."[41] Located well behind the line of a possible penetration, French forces are optimally situated to react dexterously to a crisis in which an attack from the East might be threatened. Their depth allows French forces considerable time to determine where they would most likely be needed, to decide how to deploy, to communicate with NATO and within the French command structure, and to move rapidly into position. Dexterity is important for counter–concentration in attrition warfare. In fast–paced maneuver combat, in which the defender would confront flanking actions and shifts of the focus of attack, dexterity is imperative.

The ability to carry out detection, decision, communication, and movement efficiently, both before and during a battle, is especially important given uncertainty as to when France would decide to commit its forces alongside the Allies. The essence of France's withdrawal from NATO's integrated military structure was that while it reaffirmed its commitment to European defense, it also reserved the right to determine independently the timing of its engagement in a defensive effort. It is hardly doubted that following an attack on Germany, as is commonly hypothesized, France would readily participate in combat. The more critical question is how France would react in a crisis that might lead to war.

During the 1980s, optimism about France's willingness and ability to cooperate in a crisis grew. One high–ranking American officer, formerly serving at SHAPE, expressed his conviction that as NATO moved up its scale of alert France would follow very closely, and that the necessary French political decision would come early rather than late.[42] Although French troops do not train with NATO, French commanders undergo a mapping exercise with the Alliance approximately every two years and are therefore familiar with movement schedules, where French forces would probably be needed most, and how they would be brought into a defensive operation. There may even be bilateral arrangements between France and the commander of NATO's Northern Army Group, who is a British general, for incorporation of the FAR into the defense of that region.[43] (Although France's president and foreign minister have reiterated that French troops will not be part of the newly created NATO rapid reaction corps,[44] which will contain two British divisions and will be commanded by a British general, it is not impossible to envision cooperative arrangements that would allow the FAR to work with the NATO corps in a crisis.)

However, there are at least three reasons why French forces might hesitate before joining in NATO defense. First, although the current leadership in France is strongly disposed toward close ties with the Alliance and dedicated to the goal of common West European security, it is always possible (though highly unlikely) that a future president might choose to reassert French independence, emphasizing the distinctly national aspects of Gaullist doctrine. Perhaps telling in this regard was conservative opposition to military initiatives taken by President Mitterrand prior to the outbreak of war in the Persian Gulf in 1991. Several right–wing leaders, such as Jacques Chirac and François Fillon, saw Mitterrand's decisions (for instance, sending the aircraft carrier *Clemenceau* to the Gulf, equipped with helicopters) as certain to reveal a lack of military autonomy on France's part.[45]

Second, as just mentioned, in all likelihood French forces would be called on to reinforce the northern part of Germany, the weaker half of the central region, and under NATO's current structure this would mean coming under a British commander, although technically French forces would remain under French national command. In practice, this would probably mean an arrangement such as that established in the war against Iraq, where American commanders exercised operational control over French units, which remained formally under the orders of a French general and chief of staff.[46] Unlike the officer cited above, some doubt the nature of the relationship between the British and French military. William Wallace, Deputy Director of the Royal Institute of International Affairs, notes the strong contrast between Anglo–German and Anglo–French military contacts. In the former there is a very close relationship amongst officers and soldiers alike, and for a British officer stationed in Germany to command a brigade or above he must speak German. By contrast, "British and French servicemen do not meet and work together so naturally." Deeply rooted tensions between the two countries still linger at this level of contact.[47] Therefore, France might hesitate in a crisis, out of reluctance to have troops constrained by British command or out of technical difficulties in coordinating command arrangements with the British.

Finally, the French might deliberately hesitate in deploying the First Army and FAR in order to preserve the element of tactical surprise. Not knowing where French forces would deploy would undoubtedly complicate an attacker's assault through Germany. Waiting until an assault began would allow France to confirm the geographical focus of the attack and to deploy optimally. Success of this follow–on role would require a high level of dexterity, especially as an attacker's rates of prosecution and movement are likely to increase at low force levels. The advantage of waiting must be weighed against the burden of speed and efficiency. As one French analyst notes, "Any force reduction in Central Europe that would increase the rapidity of an offense can only worry us."[48] Motivated by this concern, the French have undertaken several major initiatives to improve dexterity.

Equipment

The importance France attaches to this capability is reflected in the systems assigned priority status in the 1990–1993 program law for military equipment. In his report on the four–year plan, Defense Committee Chairman Jean–Michel Boucheron introduces the section on land forces by stressing that the bulk of funds allocated to the army over the period covered by the law will be used to enhance aeroterrestrial maneuver. (This complements the goals of the Defense Ministry's *Armées 2000* restructuring plan.) "More than in the past," he observes, "success will depend on the engagement of forces fully knowledgeable [of the battlefield], more rapidly than the adversary, and, so it seems, in close coordination with the Allies."[49] To that end, the program law devotes considerable resources to high technology battlefield observation and real time communications systems, including the *Orchidée* helicopter–based battlefield observation radar, CL 289 drone, *Brével* telecommunications missile, and fourth generation radio post (PR 4 G) for the RITA (Résau Intégré de Transmissions Automatiques) communications network. These programs, when complete, will enhance the capabilities of already deployed systems, such as the Syracuse battlefield telecommunications satellite.

Their capability for improving the efficiency of detection, decision–making, and communication will complement the versatility of the jewel in the crown of the new generation French defense technology—the *AMX–Leclerc* tank—which, when complete, will be the most sophisticated tank in the West and will excel in battlefield communications. It will possess a self–contained battle management system in the form of a data bus, it will be extremely well protected and able to perform in a contaminated environment, and it will boast a longer cannon and the ability to shoot on the move at up to 70 kilometers per hour, reloading automatically every four seconds.[50] With all of these features, combining firepower, internal intelligence receiving, survivability, and rapid mobility, the AMX–Leclerc promises to be an ideal platform for the type of warfare that could be anticipated at low force levels.

Moreover, highly mobile systems such as the AMX–Leclerc are hardly new to France and are a particularly strong element in the dexterity of French forces. As noted above, the First Army and FAR control 25 percent of attack helicopters in NATO in the ATTU. France's strong reliance on these systems is likely to pay high dividends at low force levels. One study notes that in an operational environment "in which a premium is placed on mobility, the helicopter is likely to assume an even greater tactical significance in providing reinforcement, resupply and forward insertion/descant capabilities."[51] These systems are the key to the rapid mobility of the FAR. They also perform comparatively well as anti–tank platforms, destroying ten tanks for each helicopter lost in exercises.[52] France is continuing to modernize its fleet of helicopters, for both protection/support and anti-tank missions, notably through the HAP/HAC (hélicoptère anti-protection/hélicoptère anti-char) development project in which it and Germany are cooperating.

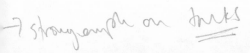

The excellent mobility provided by French helicopters is complemented by ground transport. In 1984, on the completion of a series of tests of the logistical autonomy of helicopter transport for a FAR division, France tried to apply the same concepts to land vehicles. Unlike the United States Army, the French have traditionally preferred the relatively greater maneuverability of light, wheeled vehicles over heavy, tracked tanks.[53] The result of the experiment was creation of the 6th Light Armored Division of the FAR, which would travel in a fleet of AMX 10 RCs, featuring all-terrain mobility and capable of traveling 800 kilometers without refueling, making this division, too, logistically autonomous.[54]

Operational Concept and Structure

The rapid maneuver capability associated with the equipment of the FAR matches the operational concept and structure on which that force is based. The *force d'action rapide* was conceived in the early 1980s and officially established in June 1983 under the leadership of then Defense Minister Charles Hernu. It was founded on the idea that in a crisis, France should be able to intervene rapidly beside its allies. The key qualities which should characterize such an intervention, according to Hernu, were "mobility, firepower, and flexibility."[55] Tests in 1982 indicated that the best structure for achieving this goal would be light divisions (less than 10,000 men).[56] The result was a five–division, 47,000–man *force d'action rapide*. In fact, the 6th Light Armored and the 4th Airmobile were the only newly created divisions. The 11th Paratrooper, 9th Naval Infantry and 27th Alpine divisions already existed but were unified under the FAR. In 1983 General Poirier recommended an explicit statement as to which of these divisions would be incorporated in the defense of Europe's central region and which would be withheld for other (i.e., overseas) missions. This proposal was rejected, implying, as David Yost suggests, that perhaps France intends, in a crisis, to devote the whole FAR to the NATO defense effort, but wishes to conceal that fact in peacetime.[57]

Three major dimensions can be distinguished in the operational concept of the FAR. First, as already mentioned, it should be flexible in its ability to engage in defense alongside the NATO Allies. On this subject, Hernu noted new tactical options that would be open to France through the FAR, such as the capability "to weigh in a crisis *before* it degenerates into conflict," and having a capacity for "rapid modification of land forces in the event of a surprise attack or unforeseen threat."[58] The force's flexibility has led to speculation as to how the FAR would be used in Europe. David Yost suggests that it might be assigned to security in NATO's rear.[59] Analyst Cathleen Fisher proposes four possible missions: operations on central theater flanks, security in Berlin (before unification), preparation of the theater for intervention by the Second Corps of the French First Army, and operations outside the First Army area.[60]

The second dimension of the operational concept for the FAR is surprise. As noted above, in discussing why French forces might mobilize later than forces under NATO command, there might be an important tactical advantage to be gained by keeping an attacker guessing as to where and when France would intervene. On this point Hernu made a contrast with the American analog to the FAR: "The [American] rapid deployment force would be able to enter into action only after the relatively slow mobilization of important assets, while the FAR would intervene without delay, with, of course, more limited equipment, but immediately available."[61] In the Franco–German Bold Sparrow exercise in 1987, the FAR was transported across 1200 kilometers from bases in France to positions in Germany in less than 48 hours.[62]

The final dimension of the operational concept of the FAR is its relationship to the *force de frappe*. At its inception the FAR was hailed as an effort to distinguish clearly the difference between the conventional and the prestrategic nuclear missions in the French Army. Formerly, all divisions of the army contained *Pluton* nuclear missile–equipped regiments, clouding the actual role those divisions would play. Hernu described the FAR as "independent from but complementary to the nuclear deterrent."[63] Essentially, by adding an element of uncertainty to the attacker's assumptions about French participation in Alliance defense, the FAR would increase the ambiguity surrounding the French nuclear threshold. At the same time, it would be a non–nuclear tool of crisis management in its own right. By separating the conventional and nuclear missions in this way, France further demonstrated its preference for unconstrained maneuverability in conventional defense.

Naturally, the operational concepts of flexibility, surprise capability, and independence from the nuclear force influenced the actual physical structure of the FAR. Three major innovations, already mentioned, were lightness, logistical autonomy, especially in ammunition and fuel, and all–conventional armament (i.e., no nuclear weapons). A fourth structural feature, important for flexibility, was the establishment of "liaisons with the First Army, Tactical Air Force (FATAC), and Military Air Transport Command (COTAM), as well as with the Allies."[64] Finally, the FAR's rapidity may be attributed, in large part, to its specialized, highly professional personnel.[65] Paired with the most advanced equipment, this structure and its underlying operational concept have produced an extremely maneuver–capable force. The FAR is a major pillar of French military strength and an excellent embodiment of the qualities that would be critical in combat at low force levels.

The Franco–German mixed–manned brigade, which became operational in October 1990, may also emphasize strengths similar to the FAR's. One analyst suggests possible missions for the brigade which require a high degree of mobility: "rapid establishment of blocking positions," deployment "where some firepower quickly is better than a lot later," and "rear area security."[66] This brigade may serve a symbolic and political mission. However, the concepts on which it has been designed, emphasizing cooperation and maneuverability, suggest that like the FAR it would be compatible with the type of defense best suited for Europe at low force levels.

Restructuring: *Armées 2000*

Finally, a new dimension of French military capability, which further confirms the argument that France has devoted its efforts to developing the type of maneuver defense that would become increasingly valuable for European security at extremely low force levels, is the *Armées 2000* restructuring plan, announced by Defense Minister Chevènement in June 1989. Promoted as the most extensive restructuring of French armed forces in thirty years, *Armées 2000* is intended "to lighten infrastructure, to facilitate the circulation of information, to reduce fragmentation of supports and services, to increase the clarity of command, and to intensify diligence of execution."[67] Substantively, the plan will: (1) eliminate the First Corps of the First Army, allocating its equipment and personnel to the remaining two corps and FAR; (2) move the First Army headquarters to Metz, where it will be collocated with FATAC headquarters; (3) simplify the division of the French territory into military zones, from six army, four air force, and six *gendarmerie* zones, to three large inter–force regions; (4) improve inter–force operations by establishing inter–force inspectors general (as opposed to inspectors general particular to each service) and by strengthening coordination between air and land and air and naval forces.[68]

From one point of view, this initiative is simply a way to "clean house," much as the United States did in the 1970s. Confronted with too many spaces and too few troops, the French have taken stock and tried to rationalize their military structure, so that a smaller number of units will be more capable. Alternatively, although essentially a question of reshuffling, *Armées 2000* may, in fact, improve overall operational maneuverability.

Tactical benefits could stem, first of all, from a tighter link between air and ground forces. As Henri Paris, the major exponent of *Armées 2000* in the Ministry of Defense, writes, "Henceforth, the air dimension is a common denominator, such that it is indispensable to think in terms of aeroterrestrial and aeronaval [forces]." He adds that such inter–force cadres will be best suited to exploit a wide space for maneuver and to take advantage of high technology battlefield observation provided by the *Hélios* satellite and *Orchidée* target acquisition system.[69] Coordinating and simplifying command, control and support between the two services should reduce operational friction and therefore improve dexterity. If successful, peacetime enhancement of links between air and ground forces would, ideally, allow for smooth transition from peace to crisis to war.

Furthermore, *Armées 2000* reaffirms France's commitment to cooperative defense with its European allies. This is a result of both the expected reduction in operational delays and the geographical nature of the reshuffling of forces. According to Chevènement, the decision to eliminate the First Corps at Metz rather than the Third Corps at Lille was based on the latter's "geographical location, before the northern European plains, which . . . are rather poorly covered by the northern flank of NATO's forces."[70] In other words, the main feature of the restructuring plan was based on a conscious decision to compensate for a deficiency within NATO, a potentially important step toward improving cooperation with the Alliance. While this initiative is obviously not the same as integration into NATO's military command, it does indicate an acceptance of the mission French forces would most likely be called on to fulfill. Peacetime preparation for operations in a particular direction, while not compromising the flexibility of the First Army, would enhance the efficiency of response in a crisis. It would also yield political benefits to France by reassuring Europe of French commitment.

Thus, consistent with the trend in military procurement, France's operational concepts and force structure continue to emphasize maneuverability. Not only is it able to bring a relatively large mass of force to bear, but, more important, that force is particularly well designed for the operational context that would prevail at low force levels.

At the beginning of this chapter we noted Kenneth Hunt's argument that primary reliance on nuclear weapons and the absence of a full flexible response concept in practice had largely negated the military impact of France's withdrawal from NATO's integrated military structure. If a state of East–West parity at low conventional force levels signals a return to full flexible response—primary reliance on conventional defense as the true basis of European security, not just a tripwire—then France's strong gross input of personnel and materiel, as well as the emphasis on mobility in its military structure, would assure France an important part in the new order. A return to full flexible response will also require the availability of French logistics and territorial depth, and these assets, too, would be a source of increased leverage at low force levels.

Logistics and Territorial Support

"The problem of logistics," wrote Carl Amme in 1967, "is one of the most important reasons for maintaining a substantial United States armed force in Europe."[71] If the United States were completely confident of the ability to rapidly redeploy troops to Europe, there would be no need to station more than a token force in Germany, primarily to assure the guarantee of extended nuclear deterrence. However, uncertainty as to when France would intervene with the Alliance in a crisis and the vulnerability of existing, North-South lines of communication have reduced such confidence. To hedge against the risks inherent in reinforcement from outside Europe the United States has stationed the equivalent of five and two-thirds divisions in the western part of Germany. These units could be reinforced quickly (within fifteen days) by five and one-third divisions airlifted from the United States and equipped with materiel pre-positioned in Europe (POMCUS).[72] Further reinforcements would have to be sea-lifted from the United States, entering Europe through ports in Belgium, the Netherlands, and northern

Germany (and France, once it committed its territorial assets).

As American forces withdraw from Europe, according to current and subsequent rounds of negotiations, their ability to return will become increasingly important to those who continue to perceive a potential threat to European security. (Recall our assumption about the importance of perceptions.) According to one high-ranking American officer, formerly serving at SHAPE, the United States will probably draw down, eventually, to a corps of two divisions in Europe.[73] At that stage, the ability of the United States to fulfill its commitment to European security would depend critically on assets for transporting U.S.-based units back into Europe. Joshua Epstein argues that the benefits from symmetrical East-West reductions in the ATTU after the first CFE agreement will increasingly accrue to the United States, because the American reinforcement base from outside the ATTU is considerably greater than the Soviet. Thus, "CFE II reductions . . . would magnify the asymmetrical effect of the CFE agreement. . . . The same U.S. reinforcement from the continental United States . . . looms ever larger proportionally as the numerically equal forces (tanks, artillery, and armored vehicles) within the ATTU are reduced."[74] This effect implies that assets for transporting that reinforcement safely would be readily available. Therefore, French logistical support also "looms ever larger."

In particular, French ports and rail transport would be increasingly valuable for redeployment of American forces to Europe at low force levels. David Yost observes that while Dutch and Belgian ports can handle more traffic than French ports, the accessibility of more points of entry, such as ports at Le Havre and Marseilles, would enhance the safety of reinforcement.[75] If an attacker intended to launch interdiction strikes against ports, he would now have more possible, geographically separate targets against which to send the same number of planes, and the overall kill rate would decrease accordingly. Also, additional points of entry in France would provide a degree of redundancy to hedge against the possibility that the attacker might successfully incapacitate some ports. The American officer cited above confirmed, "The last thing we want to do in reinforcing under those conditions [i.e., low force levels] would be to pack everything up into Belgium." Similarly, in his report on the 1990–1993 military program law, Jean-Michel Boucheron acknowledged, "One must not forget the importance of [French] ports on the Atlantic coast and in the Mediterranean, situated behind the probable front line, for the reinforcement of Europe." Moreover, he pointed to the critical role of the French navy in protecting those points of access and the sea lanes of communication (SLOCs) approaching Europe, since the American and British navies would probably be preoccupied in the northern and southern flanks, according to their maritime strategy.[76]

The French railroad network would further complement the logistical redundancy of multiple ports. Yost notes that this system is "too dense to be closed down easily by Soviet conventional air attack."[77] Moreover, transportation by rail across France would alleviate the problem of relying on LOCs running parallel to the probable front line. Those LOCs might be more susceptible to early disruption under the conditions of maneuver-dominated combat. The availability of logistics across France would add a valuable degree of safety.

A final important dimension of possible French territorial support is access to airfields. This too will become more critical at low force levels. As ground forces approach extremely low levels, the marginal impact of airpower on future combat would increase considerably. The added value of assuring protection of combat air forces would increase as well. Also, the imperative of safely airlifting supplies and personnel assigned to pre-positioned units would be greater as fewer American troops are stationed in Europe. As noted above, the issue of overcrowding on German air bases has concerned NATO commanders from the time of the Berlin Crisis.

These observations also apply to the nuclear element of Allied defense. As American conventional forces are being withdrawn from Germany, so are short-range nuclear forces. One idea under serious consideration in Washington is air-basing tactical nuclear weapons in the future. With this option on the table, the possibility of access to French air bases, according to one report, has become a major issue in the Pentagon.[78]

Thus the greater political leverage in shaping European security which will be associated with the "teeth" of France's military capability (its manpower and equipment) at lower force levels will be boosted by its "tail" (territorial support and logistical assets). But here a distinction must be made. In its operational units France claims to have developed the capability for rapid intervention and logistical autonomy. With little warning, or following a delayed decision, French strength could be brought to bear with little or no loss of impact than if it had been deployed early. By virtue of bulk force, influence stemming from

France's military capability would resemble the type of influence that the United States exercises in NATO today.

Logistics, by contrast, on which other nations' forces would depend, require an early decision of commitment by France, in peacetime or early in a crisis. Some observers, including the American officer cited above, believe that this would not be a problem, and that access to French LOCs, dispersal of air forces to French air bases, and other crisis-time preparations would quickly fall into place following a NATO request, according to arrangements made with the French during the 1980s. Others are more skeptical, doubting that France would compromise its independence of decision-making by committing its territory and logistical support before hostilities were clearly unavoidable. Benoit d'Aboville, a defense expert in France's Ministry of Foreign Affairs, observed that there is no question that France would dedicate its logistics to NATO in an all-out war. "The real issue," he observed, "is the case of a crisis."[79] It is imperative in a crisis that no nation appear to be taking escalatory actions. Yet skeptics would maintain that by committing its logistics to NATO before an actual war, France would be escalating a crisis and actually increasing the likelihood of such a war.

Those who doubt that a political decision to open French territory to NATO would come early in a crisis also fear that following such a decision it would take a long time to prepare logistics. By one estimate, "at least two to three weeks would be required to prepare French airfields, and a minimum of three to six weeks to prepare lines of communications across France, unless steps were taken beforehand to stock, equip, and rationalize them."[80] From this point of view, unlike the leverage associated with manpower and equipment, the leverage associated with infrastructural assets on French territory is a type of bargaining chip.

There are few, if any, doubts that French forces would intervene in a timely fashion alongside NATO. French influence in this regard would stem not from doubts, but rather from the value the rest of Western Europe would assign to such intervention. On the issue of logistics, however, French influence might stem from European doubts as to the nature of the French commitment, whether or not France intends to use this bargaining chip as such. In fact, these two types of leverage would be mutually supporting. At lower force levels, both the stable assurance of the relatively greater capability of France's military forces and the uncertainty as to the timely availability of its operationally valuable logistical assets would increase France's influence in European security.

This chapter has tried to explain why France would have greater influence in shaping the structure of European security at extremely low force levels. That case stems from a link between influence in Europe and stronger relative military capability, which continues to be relevant in today's political environment because of persistent perceptions of a threat potential, whether from a Soviet reversal or from general instability in the international system. We have seen that the dynamics of a future defense of Europe would magnify the particular advantages of French military assets and geographical position. Given the initial premise, French leverage in defining a new framework for European security should grow commensurately.

Before discussing how this newly found influence might be exercised, however, one point needs to be added. Influence in this case does not derive from the generic fact of military strength alone. In fact, in the currently evolving European security framework, a state that wielded military power but was perceived by other states as having possibly aggressive ambitions or, less extreme, was perceived as susceptible to fluctuations in its commitment to continental security might garner less influence as a result. It is precisely the stability of France's commitment, coupled with objective French strengths at low force levels, that would confer on France a relatively high degree of political leverage.

France's military program law for 1990–1993 should dispel any illusions that its commitment to European security might be flagging or inconsistent. One author suggests that, judging from authorized military expenditures, the 1990s will be for France what the 1980s were for the United States.[81] France is the only major power whose defense budget is actually increasing in real terms,[82] although relative to projections in the 1987–1991 military program, France is scaling back to a degree that some deputies consider unacceptable. This issue will be taken up in chapter four.

The French ability to maintain a consistent level of defense effort, while other European countries jealously eye a future peace dividend, may be attributed in part to French concern for multiple security threats. Thus one National Assembly deputy observed, "The threat from the East, if it is the most serious, is not the only one, and we have seen, in recent years, the development of several regional conflicts, which show us that tension remains constant."[83] Indeed, this concern was borne out by the

Persian Gulf crisis, during which France contributed substantially to the international coalition (10,500 soldiers and three naval groups). On the one hand, France's focus on global threats might seem detrimental to European security interests, to the extent that it distracts French attention. In the Gulf crisis, for instance, France acted very much independently on the diplomatic level. While calling on the Western European Union to demonstrate a solid response to the crisis, France's own actions were essentially national. In his post-war address to the nation, President Mitterrand barely mentioned Europe or the European response to the crisis, in stark contrast to other recent addresses, in which he pledged strong commitment to common West European security.[84] On the other hand, reminders of the multipolar nature of threats to French security interests allow France to sustain relatively constant allocations in its defense budget. The same light, mobile, and "smart" equipment, development and procurement of which can be justified by invoking unforeseeable threats brewing in the Third World, would be equally useful in the new European military environment.

Legislative support for constant and consistent military investment is complemented by a highly efficient and centralized military procurement process. Overseeing the process is the Délégation Générale pour l'Armement (DGA), which studies services' needs and awards industrial contracts. Efficient procurement adds ballast to the stability of the French security commitment.

Finally, it must not be forgotten that ultimately a consistent military effort is the product of a highly stable government. One problem of strategic decision-making in NATO has been that all the countries in the central region are run by coalition governments.[85] Granted, France did go through its period of cohabitation, between 1986 and 1988, when it experienced the anomaly of a Socialist president and a Gaullist (Rassemblement Pour la République-RPR) prime minister, whose responsibilities in the area of security overlap, according to the Constitution of the Fifth Republic. However, a distinguishing feature of the Fifth Republic has been the power concentrated in the office of the president. The high degree of executive centralization has been a source of efficient and stable decision-making, which should continue to reassure Europe in the future, (at least, as far as security is concerned).

Founded on a strong philosophical base, the stability of its government will be a key factor in the intra-European influence France will derive from its military strength. Political stability should provide the necessary confidence that that strength would be used to maintain balance in European security. Projecting such assurance, France will be able to derive the greatest amount of leverage in building a new European security order.

NOTES

1. Jacques Isnard, "Un entretien avec M. Chevènement," *Le Monde*, 13 July 1990, p. 9.

2. Jean Lecanuet, "Ne devançons pas la musique!" *Le Monde*, 14 July 1990, p. 2. See also Introduction, notes 7–9.

3. Jean-Pierre Chevènement in Assemblée Nationale de la République Française, "Équipement militaire pour les années 1990–1993," Débats Parlementaires, *Journal officiel de la république française*, 9e Leg., le sess., le séance, 3 October 1989, p. 3031. And Isnard, "Un entretien avec M. Chevènement."

4. See, for example, Jeanny Lorgeoux in Assemblée Nationale de la République Française, "Équipement militaire pour les années 1990–1993," Débats Parlementaires, *Journal officiel de la république française*, 9e Leg., le sess., le séance, 3 October 1989, p. 3029, and in *Journal officiel*, 2e séance, 3 October 1989, Loic Bouvard, p. 3058, and Arthur Paecht, p. 3049. Warning of reversibility is also a dominant theme in the report on the *Loi de programmation militaire, 1990–1993* by Jean-Michel Boucheron, Chairman of the Defense Commission of the National Assembly. See Assemblée Nationale de la République Française, *Rapport fait au nom de la commission de la défense nationale et des forces armées sur le projet de loi de programmation (no. 733) relatif à l'équipement militaire pour les années 1990–1993* (No. 897), Report prepared by Jean-Michel Boucheron, 9e Leg., le sess., 2 October 1989, pp. 12, 23, 46.

5. David S. Yost, *France and Conventional Defense in Central Europe* (Boulder, CO, Westview Press, 1985), p. 106. Yost's assessment might be modified by adding that beyond a certain threshold of Soviet force withdrawals, the impact of France's conventional military participation would be reduced, as NATO would be able to stalemate an offensive easily, with or without France. As long as the dynamics of warfare are simple attrition and withdrawal, French participation would prove most critical only in the marginal scenarios where NATO's ability to fend off aggression is a close call. If success or failure is clear-cut the importance of French participation naturally decreases. However, as will be discussed, at very low force levels, when maneuver rather than attrition warfare obtains, the new set of circumstances would enhance the significance of French cooperation.

6. For one scenario see Bahr, von Bülow, and Voigt, *European Security 2000—A Comprehensive Concept for European Security from a Sozial-Demokratic Point of View* (Bonn, Presservice der SPD, 6 July 1989), pp. 2–4. The "Comprehensive Concept" delineates the following hardware limits for each alliance in the ATTU: 9,080 battle tanks, 2,100 mechanized infantry combat vehicles, 21,020 armored personnel carriers, 8,850 tube artillery, mortars or rocket launchers, 765 assault and anti-tank helicopters.

7. Robert McNamara in U.S. Congress, Senate, Combined Subcommittee of Foreign Relations and Armed Services Committees on the Subject of United States Troops in Europe, *United States Troops in Europe*, Hearing before the Combined Subcommittee of Foreign Relations and Armed Services Committees on the Subject of United States Troops in Europe, 90th Cong., 1st Sess., 26 April and 3 May 1967, pp. 25–26.

8. Chet Holifield, *Improving NATO Nuclear Weapon Planning*, Statement (3 May 1966). NB: All historical documents used in this study are available at the National Security Archive, 1755 Massachusetts Ave., NW, Suite 500, Washington, DC 20036. This will be indicated henceforth as "NSA."

9. Waldo Drake, "NATO Faces Necessity of Regrouping," *Los Angeles Times*, 8 December 1957, p. 1. NSA.

10. Brigadier Kenneth Hunt, *NATO without France: The Military Implications*, Adelphi Paper, 32 (London, The Institute for Strategic Studies, December 1966), p. 10.

11. Carl H. Amme, Jr., *NATO without France: A Strategic Appraisal* (Stanford, Stanford University Press, 1967), p. 158. Amme noted that "no additional European contribution will make up for the net reduction."

12. Hunt, p. 11.

13. Hunt, p. 10.

14. Stuart Symington in U.S. Congress, Senate, Combined Subcommittee of Foreign Relations and Armed Services Committees on the Subject of United States Troops in Europe, *United States Troops in Europe*, Hearing before the Combined Subcommittee of Foreign Relations and Armed Services Committees on the Subject of United States Troops in Europe, 90th Cong., 1st Sess., 26 April and 3 May 1967, pp. 50–51.

15. Amme, p. 70.

16. Hunt, p. 15.

17. Amme, p. 87.

18. Interview in late February 1990. [This information was provided on a non-attribution basis.] Information provided by this officer has been extremely helpful to the writing of the current work. He is referred to in the text as "a high-ranking American officer formerly serving at SHAPE."

19. Hunt, p. 1.

20. Hunt, p. 12.

21. Col. B. K. Yount, U.S. Department of Defense, Office of the Assistant Secretary of Defense for International Security Affairs, European Region, *Emergency Authority to Stockpile Atomic Weapons in France*, Memorandum for Vice President's Visit to Paris, 29–30 September 1961 (27 September 1961). NSA.

22. Amme, p. 117.

23. Amme, p. 69.

24. Hunt, p. 10.

25. The International Institute for Strategic Studies, *The Military Balance, 1990–1991* (London, Pergamon-Brassey's for IISS, 1990), p. 232. Note, however, that estimates of French manpower vary. See, for example, "La Défense en Chiffres 1990," *Armées d'Aujourd'hui*, Supplement au no. 147 (February 1990). According to this source, manpower devoted to French ground forces totals approximately 220,000 (excluding civilians). This would naturally reduce the combined total for ground and air forces.

26. Helmut Schmidt, "Europe Should Begin to Assert Itself, and the French Should Take the Lead," translation in *World Press Review* (February 1987), p. 23.

27. U.S. Arms Control and Disarmament Agency, Office of Public Affairs, *CFE: Negotiation on Conventional Armed Forces in Europe* (Washington, DC, U.S. Arms Control and Disarmament Agency, Office of Public Affairs, 31 August 1990).

28. "Britain to Cut Force in Germany by Half," *The New York Times*, 26 July 1990, p. A8.

29. See, for example, Isnard, "Un entretien avec M. Chevènement."

30. "L'allocution télévisé du Président de la République," *Le Monde*, 5 March 1990, p. 6.

31. Klaus Peter Moller, cited in André Brigot, "Enduring Issues in Franco-German Relations," in Philippe G. Le Prestre, ed., *French Security Policy in a Disarming World* (Boulder, CO, Lynne Rienner Publishers, 1989), p. 91.

32. The International Institute for Strategic Studies, *The Military Balance, 1989–1990* (London, Pergamon-Brassey's for IISS, 1989), p. 239. However, if this statistic is accurate, then for the figure cited in note 31 to be true there will have to be a long-term decline in birth rate. In other words, the relatively high conscript pool in 1996 must ultimately decline if the overall population will remain constant in 2025.

33. Pierre Lellouche, "Rebuild or Decay: The Future of the European Security System (A French Perspective)," in Stanley R. Sloan, ed., *NATO in the 1990s* (Washington, DC, Pergamon-Brassey's, 1989), p. 256.

34. "Comparison of CFE Declarations and Residual Ceilings," reprinted in *Survival* (January/February 1991), p. 83. Note that in this and following categories estimates vary. According to *The Military Balance, 1990–1991*,

France has 242 attack helicopters (i.e., SA-341s and SA-342s equipped for combat), as compared to NATO's total of 1,005 in the ATTU. See also Claire Tréan, "100,000 pièces à la casse," *Le Monde*, 20 November 1990, p. 3. According to this source, the NATO helicopter total is 1,650, and it is reported that France will withdraw 87 rather than 77 of its helicopters.

35. "Comparison of CFE Declarations and Residual Ceilings." According to estimates reprinted here, France owns 4,125 armored combat vehicles, compared to a NATO total of 34,453. France will reduce to 3,820, while NATO as a whole will reduce to 29,822. However, once again estimates vary. The figure of 16 percent for France in the central region, cited in the text, is derived from *The Military Balance, 1990–1991*, which assigns France 4,846 armored combat vehicles and NATO 29,465 in the area of the central region and France and 43,674 in the ATTU.

36. "Comparison of CFE Declarations and Residual Ceilings." This source lists France's current combat air power as 700, compared to a NATO total of 5,939 in the ATTU. *The Military Balance, 1990–1991* estimates French combat aircraft at 579, compared to a NATO total of 4,884. See also Air Vice-Marshal R. A. Mason, "Airpower in Conventional Arms Control," *Survival* (September/October 1989), pp. 398–99, 402. This source assigns France 450 combat aircraft and NATO 5,037, based on NATO, "The Facts," 25 November 1988. Finally, according to "La Défense en Chiffres 1990," 180 French aircraft are designated for air defense, and 270 are designated for tactical nuclear (prestrategic) missions.

37. This analysis is derived from Joshua M. Epstein, *Conventional Force Reductions* (Washington, DC, The Brookings Institution, 1990), Appendix C. This appendix provides an extensive accounting of all NATO and WTO forces that would be available for Central Europe, their likely times of arrival at the front, and their respective WUV scores. For a discussion of WEI/WUV accounting, Epstein cites Williams, Weapons Effectiveness Indices/Weighted Unit Values (WEI/WUV) III Study Report CAA-SR-79-12 (U.S. Army Concepts Analysis Agency, 1979; declassified, 1986).

38. Epstein. Appendices A and B contain the equations of the Adaptive Dynamic Model and a discussion of their derivation.

39. Paul K. Davis, Robert D. Howe, Richard L. Kugler, and William G. Wild, Jr., *Variables Affecting Central Region Stability: The "Operational Minimum" and Other Issues at Low Force Levels*, RAND Note N-2976-USDP (Santa Monica, The RAND Corp., 1989), p. 46.

40. Benoit d'Aboville, interview at the French Consulate, New York, NY, 8 January 1990.

41. Epstein, p. 14.

42. Interview, non-attributable (see this chapter, note 18).

43. This idea was suggested by the officer cited in note 18, though he

stressed that this was only speculation.

44. See introduction, note 10.

45. See François Fillon, "Mais à quoi sert le 'Clemenceau'?" *Le Monde*, 8 September 1990, p. 2, and Jacques Chirac, cited in Jean-Yves Lhomeau, "L'exercice solitaire de la décision," *Le Monde*, 22 January 1991, p. 13.

46. Jacques Isnard, "Vingt-neuf pays face à une forteresse," *Le Monde*, 16 January 1991, p. 4.

47. William Wallace, "European Security: Bilateral Steps to Multilateral Co-operation," in Yves Boyer, Pierre Lellouche, and John Roper, eds., *Franco-British Defence Co-operation* (London, Royal Institute of International Affairs, 1988), p. 178.

48. André Brigot, "A Neighbor's Fears: Enduring Issues in Franco-German Relations," in Le Prestre, ed., p. 92.

49. Assemblée Nationale de la République Française, *Rapport fait au nom de la commission de la défense nationale et des forces armées sur le projet de loi de programmation (no. 733) relatif à l'équipement militaire pour les années 1990–1993*, No. 897, Report prepared by Jean-Michel Boucheron, 9e Leg., le sess., 2 October 1989, p. 262 (hereafter referred to as Boucheron, *Rapport*).

The military program law (*loi de programmation militaire*) is a five-year defense plan. It carries more weight than guidelines, since it actually legislates defense spending for five years. A program law was passed in 1986 to cover the period 1987–1991. However, the Socialist Party has regained a majority in the National Assembly since then, and in 1989 proposed a new program law to cover the period 1990–1993, on the grounds that the 1987–1991 law was too ambitious. The main bone of contention was Title V spending, which covers procurement and research, development and testing of equipment. The 1990–1993 law, which was accepted in October 1989, allocates 437.8 billion francs to Title V over the period covered by the law.

50. Boucheron, *Rapport*, p. 269, and Lt. Col. John S. Westerlund, "The French Army of the 1990s," *Military Review* (February 1990), p. 42.

51. Mason, p. 411. Similarly, in 1967 Amme observed, "If the emphasis is on crisis management, it would appear that a flight of helicopters could do as well as a platoon of heavy tanks, particularly where quick action is essential to snuff out a conflict or to prevent a *fait accompli*." See Amme, p. 147.

52. Cited in Yves Boyer, "The U.S. Military Presence in Europe and French Security Policy," *The Washington Quarterly* (Spring 1988), p. 205.

53. Westerlund, p. 41.

54. Lt. Col. Jean-François Louvion, *The French Rapid Action Force: A Key Element in European Continental Defense*, research report (Maxwell Air Force Base, AL, Air University, 1988), p. 18.

55. Charles Hernu, *Défendre la paix* (Paris, J. C. Lattès, 1985), p. 60.

56. Louvion, pp. 16–17.

57. Yost, p. 90.

58. Hernu, pp. 62–63.

59. Yost, p. 91.

60. Cathleen Fisher, "Franco-German Cooperation in Conventional Force Planning," in Robbin F. Laird, ed., *Strangers and Friends: The Franco-German Security Relationship* (London, Pinter Publishers, 1989), p. 78.

61. Hernu, p. 71.

62. Robert Grant, "French Security Policy and the Franco-German Relationship," in Laird, ed., *Strangers and Friends*, p. 27.

63. Hernu, p. 74.

64. Louvion, p. 18.

65. Boucheron, *Rapport*, p. 259.

66. Westerlund, p. 41.

67. Henri Paris, "Les armées de l'an 2000," *Défense Nationale* (November 1989), p. 41. Henri Paris is a very highly placed official in the Ministry of Defense and has been the prime articulator of *Armées 2000*.

68. Ministère de la Défense de la République Française, *Armées 2000* (Paris, Ministère de la Défense de la République Française, 26 July 1989), pp. 1–2.

69. Paris, pp. 37–38.

70. Jean-Pierre Chevènement in Audition de M. Jean-Pierre Chevènement, Réunion du mardi 10 juin 1989, in Boucheron, *Rapport*, p. 730.

71. Amme, p. 87.

72. Epstein, Appendix C.

73. Interview, non-attributable (see note 18).

74. Epstein, p. 49.

75. Yost, pp. 59–60, 64.

76. Boucheron, *Rapport*, pp. 330, 331.

77. Yost, p. 66.

78. Michael Brenner, "Une nouvelle optique sur la sécurité européene: Le regard de Washington," *Politique Étrangère* (no. 3, 1990), p. 553.

79. d'Aboville, interview (see this chapter, note 40).

80. Robert Komer, cited in Yost, p. 75.

81. Westerlund, p. 37.

82. Cited by André Bellon in Assemblée Nationale de la République Française, "Équipement militaire pour les années 1990–1993," 2e séance, 3 October 1989, p. 3067.

83. Philippe Mestre in Assemblée Nationale de la République Française, "Équipement militaire pour les années 1990–1993," 1e séance, 3 October 1989, p. 3062. See also, Boucheron, *Rapport*, p. 95.

84. "L'allocution télévisée du président de la République," p. 6.

85. Interview with high-ranking American officer, formerly at SHAPE (see note 18).

CHAPTER 3

A FRENCH CONCEPT FOR THE FUTURE OF EUROPEAN SECURITY

Thus far, we have looked at major factors pointing to a strong French role in shaping a new European security order. Based on those factors and on trends in current French policy, it should be possible to describe how such an order would reflect France's influence. Before proceeding, however, a brief recapitulation is in order, as the strength of the points to be made in this chapter necessarily rests on the coherence of the argument presented earlier.

First, the rapid transformation in the structure of East-West political relations has shaken the foundation of the Atlantic Alliance, such that Western Europe is more susceptible today than at any time in the past 25 years to a redefinition of the bases of security. The catalyst for such a redefinition is the prospect of extremely low conventional force levels in Europe. This new reality will alter relative strengths of member countries in NATO, while disclosing fundamental differences in interpretation of the doctrines (flexible response, in particular) that have supported NATO institutions since 1967. The inability of institutions to absorb such rapid change and respond coherently could be crippling.

Second, tension between cooperation and integration as basic concepts of European security animated debate in the Atlantic Alliance during the 1960s and may return as an important theme in the debate of the 1990s. Cooperation, as encouraged by France under the leadership of de Gaulle, implies a traditional security alliance based on a mutual

promise of autonomous members to defend one another, but requiring
minimal peacetime institutional structure. Integration, as encouraged
by the United States, entails extensive institutionalization of peacetime
planning on political as well as strategic issues. Even with France's
withdrawal from the integrated military structure in 1966 and the
adoption of flexible response and the Harmel Report in 1967, it was
not clear that a permanent solution founded on one or the other concept
had been achieved. Despite their apparent robustness, the American-led
institutions that grew up in NATO over two decades were based on
ambiguous compromise rather than consensus. By revealing the fault
lines that underlie "acceptance" of integration, massive conventional
force reductions promise to reopen the integration-cooperation debate.

Third, the primary exponent of cooperation, France, will hold considerable leverage in shaping security at extremely low force levels.
While the idea of a future war in Europe seems highly unlikely,
the perception amongst leaders and populations of instability and
uncertainty in the current security environment and the inertia of cold
war thinking support the continued relevance of stable military strength.
The Gulf war and Soviet use of force in repressing popular movements
in the Baltic republics have helped to revalue military capability. A
non-aggressive power with a consistent level of political commitment
to Western Europe, a defense designed for the security environment
likely to evolve in the future, and territorial infrastructure which could
become critical for defense of the continent, France should look forward
to a new degree of diplomatic influence among its neighbors.

If one accepts the first and third points—that European security is
ripe for a major redefinition and that France's relative weight within
the system is growing (and that there continues to be a strong link
between stable military strength and influence in shaping security
arrangements)—then the simple conclusion that France currently has
a historic opportunity to establish a position of leadership in European
security should follow. But one might still ask why the integration-
cooperation dichotomy is the proper context in which to analyze the
expression of that leadership. After all, much has changed in the
relationships between France and NATO and between France and the
United States since 1966.

Even after its withdrawal, France remained an active participant in
most NATO institutions, with the notable exceptions of the Defense
Planning Committee and the Nuclear Planning Group, and over the

course of 25 years it has gradually drawn nearer to the Alliance. Arrangements have been made to ensure close coordination between French and Alliance responses in a crisis. One high-ranking American officer, formerly serving at SHAPE, who has watched closely the transformation of French security policy since de Gaulle firmly maintains his conviction that in a crisis today, France would follow NATO up the scale of alert. The French chief of staff would be in constant communication with SACEUR. A political decision to commit French forces and support to the Alliance would come early, and the plans activated pursuant to such a decision would be all-encompassing— logistics as well as forces would fall into line. Furthermore, he asserts, this coordination would apply to nuclear weapons as well as to conventional defense.[1] Clearly the France of the 1990s is not the France of 1966. Why, then, should an analysis of the new French influence in European security refer to the historical debate on the nature of security?

The answer to this question lies in the relative strength and stability over time of the Gaullist tenets of the Fifth Republic. While the emphasis in French security policy has varied at different moments in the 1970s and 1980s between Atlanticism and Europeanism and between nationalism and supranationalism, leaders have consistently grounded their policies in the doctrines of General de Gaulle. Thus, for instance, President François Mitterrand invariably invokes France's "rank" in his addresses to the nation.[2] Mitterrand's policies have been described as a "neo-Gaullism of the Left."[3] Throughout his *Réflexions sur la politique extérieure de la France*, a personal account of his thoughts on France's foreign policy from 1981 to 1985, Mitterrand evokes Gaullist themes. He reminds the reader that, although formerly opposed to a strategy based on nuclear deterrence, he led the Socialist Party in 1978 to acceptance of the Gaullist doctrine of *faible au fort* (proportional deterrence). He stresses the importance of autonomy in French military decisions, which he affirms is preserved in the *force d'action rapide*. Most important for the current discussion, Mitterrand, like de Gaulle, argues that "France's independence and the construction of Europe are mutually complementary."[4] As Mitterrand expressed this formula in 1987, *"La France est ma patrie; l'Europe, c'est mon avenir."*[5] These are the very ideals that, now as in the 1960s, distinguish cooperation from integration in the French vision of European security.

In France today the themes of the 1960s security debate continue to figure largely. (In fact, as will be argued in chapter four, the imperative of justifying French policy according to Gaullist doctrine may be more constraining than empowering.) It is reasonable to discuss the dimensions of French influence in shaping the future of security in Europe in terms of a dichotomy between cooperation and integration. While the leadership style in France has changed, the philosophical underpinnings of the Fifth Republic are relatively constant. As Western European security based on integration appears to be faltering, and as French influence grows, France may be expected, accordingly, to press for the creation of a new order around the model of cooperation without integration, which has been a trademark of French security in the Fifth Republic. This chapter will sketch the main dimensions that would characterize such an order.

COOPERATION OVER INTEGRATION

In an opinion which appeared in *Le Monde* in early March 1990, author Jean-Paul Pigasse applauded a statement by Defense Minister Chevènement calling for "the emergence of a true European defense pillar." He interpreted Chevènement's words as signalling the return of the European Defense Community, abandoned by France's National Assembly in 1954, and cheered, *"La CED enfin!"* (Finally, the EDC!) "The Minister of Defense having lifted the taboo [of the Gaullist dogma of military independence]," wrote Pigasse, "France must take giant strides along the route of military integration of Europe."[6] I cite this point of view for purposes of contrast, to illustrate the type of regime which is likely *not* to evolve under French leadership. The French National Assembly rejected the EDC in 1954 precisely because it was so highly integrative; for the same reasons, such an organization is likely to be rejected today.

The EDC's proposed mandate had called for "as complete an integration as possible . . . within a supranational European organization." To that end, member nations would have dedicated prescribed levels of personnel and materiel to the European Defense Forces. National forces not committed to the EDC would have been limited, according to article ten of the EDC Treaty. Soldiers in the Community would have worn a common uniform (article 15) and would have "depended for their existence and maintenance upon higher integrated echelons" (articles 68 and 69). The EDC Treaty had established a Commissariat,

Council, Assembly and Court which would have governed all defense-related activities in Europe, including military industries and trade in war materiel with parties inside and outside Europe (article 107).[7] A network so extensive and so tightly integrated obviously conflicted with the French concept of security which would be articulated by de Gaulle on his return to power, four years after the abandonment of the EDC. The EDC would have restricted national autonomy in defense-related decision-making to a degree unacceptable in France. It represented an ideal type of integration, diametrically opposed to the French vision of cooperation.

The assessment that by proclaiming French support for a "true European pillar of defense" the Defense Minister signalled a new era in which France henceforth is amenable to the philosophy of the European Defense Community is fundamentally flawed. That conclusion ignores a basic tension at the root of French security policy, which tends to favor cooperation over integration. That is the tension between nationalism and Europeanism.

Mitterrand's statements make clear that he thinks it should be possible, from a Gaullist perspective, to have both nationalism and Europeanism. How the two can be achieved simultaneously has always been ambiguous. This dilemma was the essence of France's ambivalence in the MLF debate. More recently, it was at the heart of France's initially vague position on the question of German unification. As French scholar Alfred Grosser observes, "The future of East Germany is an uncomfortable subject for the French. It is not discussed openly because it raises the issue of national sovereignty versus the emerging Continent of Europe."[8] Another author laments,

Between the ideology of the national state . . . and the practice of a policy unifying . . . the European nations in the construction of European independence, the French leaders and the French voters have never known how to choose. . . . One dreams what might have happened if General de Gaulle had devoted the end of his life to telling the people of France that, henceforth, their sole ambition should be the construction of Greater Europe, which alone in the 21st Century would prevent our children and our grand-children from becoming servile and passive subjects of extra-European world powers. But this was not to be.[9]

The tension between nationalism and Europeanism, alive today as it was in the 1960s, has yielded the French preference for cooperation rather than integration in European security and precludes for the foreseeable future, a return to the EDC. Since early 1990, France's leaders have begun to clarify the French concept of a European defense pillar. Referring to the NATO summit declaration of July 1990, then Defense Minister Chevènement agreed with the conclusion that the "new" Alliance should adopt a political emphasis, but he added that it should be characterized more by contribution and cooperation than by integration.[10]

If the first observation to be made about future French influence in a European security order is that it will stress cooperation over integration, the second key observation is that it will probably not focus on any one particular organization. In other words, French leadership will not encourage structuring security according to a hierarchy, for example, of NATO over the Western European Union or the WEU over the Conference on Security and Cooperation in Europe. Unlike the United States, which has exercised its leadership essentially through NATO institutions, France is likely to develop its leadership in security at several different levels. Foreign Minister Roland Dumas alluded to such a distinction in an address before the Institut des hautes études de défense nationale (IHEDN), during which he remarked, "We are passing from a bipolar, fractured world, where systems of cooperation and solidarity were rivals, to a less rigid system, in which systems of solidarity will complement each other."[11] Similarly, as Chevènement stated, "We can envision a Europe consisting of concentric circles, in which the countries of the East, on the road of democratization, would be associated with the EEC."[12]

While both statements are relatively vague, they suggest a starting point for defining the broad features of a European security order based on a multi-dimensional, cooperative approach. In particular, the image of circles provides a useful framework in which to discuss the various dimensions. Although President Mitterrand has yet to put forward a definitive French blueprint for European security—he has spoken of a European confederation but has not defined this term—it is possible to extrapolate from the information available, including statements by French political leaders and scholars, four circles which would characterize a new Europe based on the French model. These circles should be thought of as overlapping rather than concentric, as there does not seem to be a hierarchy among them. They are, in no particular order: NATO, the Franco-German "special relationship," the Western

European Union/European Community, and a European confederation (i.e., a new concert of Europe linking East and West). Each of these institutions already exists in one form or another. However, except for NATO, they have all been relatively dormant.

In the American concept of European security all other levels of interaction are subordinate to NATO. Thus, while Secretary of State Baker, in his "Architecture for a New Era" address in Berlin (December 1989), spoke of new roles for the EC and the CSCE, he also called for an expanded NATO agenda, including: establishment of a "NATO arms control verification staff," consultation on regional conflicts, and consultation on "economic and political ties with the East."[13] As might have been expected, French reaction to Baker's recommendations was mixed. Notably, the French questioned Baker's strong adherence to NATO for functions which they see as more applicable to the CSCE process.[14] A similar French reaction followed the American Secretary of State's affirmation at the June 1991 NATO foreign ministers meeting that NATO should remain "the principal means of consultation and the place for elaboration of all policies affecting the security of its members."[15]

The French concept would more likely attach equal importance to all four levels of European security. Statements by French leaders since the end of 1989 have proposed elevating the status of the Franco-German relationship, the European Community/Western European Union, and an evolving pan-European forum (currently in the CSCE framework). In a French-led order, each of these three systems, along with NATO, would carry approximately equal weight. The different dimensions would overlap, although each would serve distinct purposes.

NATO

France continues to see a need for the Atlantic Alliance, which would have an integral role to play in the French concept of a European security order. Its primary function would be to preserve an American link to the defense of the continent. President Mitterrand observed in 1986, "The worst danger for us would be that the Americans move away from the shores of our continent."[16] Indeed, the Mitterrand era has marked a strengthening of the French rapprochement with the Alliance—a rapproachment that actually began during de Gaulle's presidency.

Shortly after France's withdrawal from NATO's military command, the Ailleret-Lemnitzer agreement (named for the chief of France's armed forces and the SACEUR at the time) established contingency arrangements for French cooperation with the Allies in a crisis. This was supplemented in 1974 by the Valentin-Ferber agreement. In the 1970s there was increased French participation in NATO exercises, and in 1976, under the presidency of Valery Giscard d'Estaing, General Guy Méry articulated the policy of "enlarged sanctuarization," whereby France would consider German territory to be within its vital interests and would commit itself to participation in a forward battle even if France still would not station troops forward in peacetime.[17] The establishment of the FAR in 1983, enhancing France's capability to join rapidly in a conventional defense of Western Europe, was interpreted in NATO as one of the strongest indications thus far of France's drawing closer to the Alliance's military structure.

One might counter that since November 1989 the European security environment has changed radically, probably irreversibly, and that, therefore, it may not be inappropriate to cite earlier French overtures toward NATO as evidence of a continued French interest in the Atlantic Alliance. If France truly favors cooperation over integration, given the opportunity to alter the shape of security, it might be expected to encourage the replacement of NATO, the archetypical, existing example of integration, with a different regime entirely. In fact, until March 1990 it was not clear what status French policy would assign NATO in the future.

It became evident early in the Cold War that in shaping European security the critical stake in the balance would be Germany. In the historical debate between integration and cooperation, the United States and France had each been trying to win over Germany to its respective concept. Similarly, in 1990, as the German question loomed larger, the basic issue for NATO's future was whether a unified Germany would be integrated in the Alliance. Without Germany, NATO's continued viability would be doubtful. Although the Alliance did exist for five years before the Federal Republic was invited to join, the Alliance's evolution since 1954, and particularly after the adoption of flexible response, has made Germany's membership virtually indispensable.

The French position on the future status of a unified Germany was extremely vague until March 1990. In the weeks following the opening of the Berlin Wall, President Mitterrand was initially praised in France as somewhat of a prophet for having declared a week before the event, "I am not afraid of reunification. History marches on; I accept it for what it is. I think that the desire for reunification is legitimate for the Germans."[18] Yet despite his foresight and the boldness of his rhetoric, Mitterrand was slow to define a concrete French response. As late as February 1990, at the *Wehrkunde* conference of NATO defense ministers, one reporter observed that Chevènement "placed German neutrality and reunification within NATO back to back and found them equally destabilizing."[19] In all likelihood, France was concerned that either alternative would compromise its leadership in Europe. Insistence on neutrality might antagonize relations with Bonn and, more important, exacerbate perceptions of instability in the form of a loose Germany on the deck of Europe. On the other hand, by supporting unified Germany within NATO, France probably feared weakening a good relationship with the Soviet Union and the leverage it might exercise through the Paris-Moscow axis.

However, on 1 March, in an address before the West Berlin Press club, Foreign Minister Roland Dumas finally announced the definitive French policy on German reunification and, *de facto*, on the future of NATO. This policy rejected neutrality and supported unified Germany's integration in NATO.[20] Dumas emphasized this point again, two weeks later, in an essay in the *New York Times*, in which he asserted, "The Atlantic Alliance reflects common values and the sense of belonging to the same sphere of security. This is why I hope a unified Germany becomes part of the Alliance. This is its natural place. . . . Trans-Atlantic ties and the American presence in Europe," he added, "must continue to be recognized as key elements in the future stability of our continent."[21]

The importance France continues to attach to the Alliance was reflected in discussions on withdrawal of the French II Corps from Baden, Germany, where it is currently stationed. Addressing the nation in mid-July 1990, President Mitterrand stressed that France's decision would not be made without consulting its Allies.[22] Later, Chevènement stated that French troops would be off German soil by 1994. Mitterrand modified this statement at the time of his summit with Chancellor Kohl in September. Instead of announcing a full withdrawal, he decided that French forces stationed in Germany would be halved within two years. As one observer proposes, this modification may have been inspired by concern that total withdrawal of stationed forces could have a domino effect, ending with a total American pullout, which France does not want.[23]

If maintenance of the Alliance as a "key element of stability" would be a priority in a French-shaped security order, one might ask how this dimension would be reconciled with elevation to a more active status of the other three overlapping circles, each of which would be relatively much less integrated than NATO is today. The answer lies, once again, in the difference between the French and American concepts of the Alliance. In a radio interview in January 1990, Chevènement commented, "We are against blocs, but not necessarily against [the NATO and Warsaw Pact] alliances, as long as they move toward the reduction of stationed forces."[24] The distinction the French make between "bloc" and "alliance" corresponds to the distinction between integration and cooperation respectively. So, while the fact of American commitment to Europe through NATO is still essential, the level of actual American military presence in Europe, according to the French view, should decrease to the point where NATO becomes an alliance, rather than a bloc.

Remaining an alliance rather than a bloc also means that NATO "should not give the impression that it is seeking to take advantage of the changes in recent years in East-West relations in order to extend its military role." This was the word of caution that Foreign Minister Roland Dumas offered to NATO's foreign ministers at Copenhagen (6 June 1991). The implication is that NATO in the aftermath of the Cold War should not look for a role in Eastern Europe or other so-called "out-of-area" regions.[25] It was with this in mind that President Mitterrand expressed reservations following the May 28–29 1991 NATO defense ministers meeting, at which it was decided to restructure integrated forces.[26] A bloc might tread on terrain that would be more appropriately managed by a unified Western European security organization or by the CSCE.

The events of 1989–1990 inspired strategists and political leaders to offer some definition of the possible features of an Alliance reformed in the French image. Former President Valery Giscard d'Estaing called for transformation of the Atlantic Pact into a Euro-Atlantic Pact.[27] France would re-enter into this military structure, in which privileges and responsibilities would be redistributed. Former Defense Minister André Giraud foresaw a NATO with a separate European branch, responsible to a European political authority but coordinated with

American command. According to this image, national forces would remain loosely connected to a permanent structure, as France's are today, while small multi-national units could exist.[28] Former Chief of Armed Forces General François Valentin envisioned a similar arrangement. He described a regime in which there would be no forces stationed outside of national territory except for small multi-national units that would guard depots, bases, air defense sites, and other infrastructural assets, which would remain available in Germany. The Alliance would be loosely constructed but would be able to revert to tight integration in a crisis.[29]

The preference for more flexible cooperation would seem to imply a dismantling of many of the integrated policy-making institutions which proliferated in NATO after France withdrew from the military structure. One analyst speaks of this reform as a "remilitarization" of NATO, in the sense that its sole task would be "the eventual defense of its members, to the exclusion of all other political missions."[30] In contrast to the broad scope and tighter integration that developed in NATO over 25 years, "defense and security are serious enough matters for NATO to busy itself on these issues," notes another analyst, "especially at a time when there is a need for so many adjustments. Giving NATO a much wider agenda will divert energy from its main purpose and eventually turn NATO into a talk shop with diminishing military relevancy."[31] Another observer finds that "even if NATO invents for itself new, more cooperative, more political, more preventive functions, this will not constitute a reason for existence as powerful as was the Soviet threat."[32] The new givens, in the French view, demand a more balanced division of labor.

BI-NATIONAL COOPERATION: THE FRANCO-GERMAN SPECIAL RELATIONSHIP

The second dimension of a French-shaped security order, tighter Franco-German coupling, would be closely linked with NATO, in that it too would serve as a measure to root Germany firmly in Europe. However, from there the functional paths of the two systems would diverge. While NATO would be a leaner institution, a traditional alliance in which commitments would be limited to the mutual defense promise of article five of the North Atlantic Treaty, the bi-national level of security (beginning with the Franco-German couple, but eventually expanding to include other cooperative dyads in Western Europe) might absorb many of the policy-making responsibilities that have until now filled NATO's broad agenda. Joint positions on arms control and verification, for instance, would more likely be formulated at the bilateral or all–West European level of security cooperation than at the NATO level, especially as American forces draw down to very low numbers. Peacetime force planning, multi-national exercises, and other integrative activities of which France has been wary in a forum of sixteen, could become the substance of a growing set of cooperative arrangements between two neighbors, in which the decision-making autonomy of each would still be largely preserved.

The Franco-German security relationship is based on the Elysée Accord, signed by President de Gaulle and Chancellor Adenauer in January 1963. The main operative clauses of the Treaty call for consultation between the two countries on strategy and tactics, exchange of personnel, joint efforts in armaments production, and collaboration in civil defense.[33] The status of the Franco-German relationship vis-à-vis NATO has historically combined both antagonistic and complementary elements. Undoubtedly, at the time, de Gaulle had intended for the newly kindled friendship to constitute an alternative locus of security arrangements in Europe, distinct from the American model. Yet, in ratifying the Treaty, the German Bundestag insisted on adding a unilateral preamble, declaring Germany's continued commitment to the United States, to Europe and to the Alliance. This came as a blow to de Gaulle's design, and, disheartened by the preamble, the General declared the Treaty effectively weakened.

Over two decades the Elysée Accord became an agreement more in principle than in substance. Then in 1982, through extended consultations between French and German foreign affairs and defense officials, it was reactivated. A Council of Foreign and Defense Ministers was created, as well as a subministerial group meeting four times annually. The three committees of this group study political and strategic issues, operational tactical issues, and arms production cooperation, respectively. The trend toward greater security cooperation between France and Germany continued throughout the 1980s. In 1986, President Mitterrand and Chancellor Kohl announced plans to expand further their countries' joint defense effort. They called for common officers' education and the study of efficient incorporation of French troops into German territory during a crisis, and the French president pledged to consult his German counterpart on the launching of prestrategic nuclear weapons during a crisis or war. In 1988 a protocol was added to the Elysée Accord on its 25th anniversary, establishing joint exercises, joint officer training, a Franco-German Council for Defense and Security, and a mixed-manned Franco-German brigade, which had been proposed by Chancellor Kohl in 1987.[34]

France and Germany held their first major joint military maneuvers in September 1987 with the Bold Sparrow exercise in southwest Germany. Bold Sparrow combined 55,000 German and 20,000 French troops, the latter mostly from the 4th Airmobile and 6th Light Armored Divisions of the FAR. Then Defense Minister André Giraud praised the undertaking as "a concrete manifestation of common will animating France and the FRG to reinforce their cooperation in the matter of security and to promote a true European pillar of defense."[35] Others were more skeptical, pointing to the lack of realism in the way the exercise was conducted. These critics noted, for example, that by using only the FAR, which can move rapidly but cannot hold territory for any length of time, France's part in the simulation proved very little.[36]

Similar criticism has been directed against the mixed-manned Franco-German brigade, which was officially activated in December 1988 and became operational in October 1990. Some analysts have observed that the brigade will be basically a political symbol, as it will draw on non-essential forces of the two nations. They point out that, strictly speaking, it is not really "mixed," because each of the four regiments and three companies is either French or German.[37]

The perspective within the French and German military establishments is, expectedly, much different. Contrary to the criticism noted above, the secretaries of the Franco-German Defense and Security Council, meeting in early 1990, reported that the mixed brigade could well serve as a model for the creation of other multi-national units in Europe.[38] Supporters point out that, in contrast to the NATO structure, it is not only the command of the mixed brigade, but the units themselves that are integrated. Day-to-day problems such as equipment inter-operability and discipline, according to this point of view, are confronted more directly in this framework than in NATO's layer cake forward defense structure, where each nation is responsible for its own corps sector in Germany.[39]

Along with tighter peacetime integration of some forces, France has accepted in its relationship with its neighbor a wider agenda for common decision-making than in its relationship with its fifteen Allies. The Franco-German Council for Defense and Security, which met for the first time on 20 April 1989, is tasked with "the establishment of common concepts in the area of defense and security, and the development of planning on all questions concerning the security of Europe."[40] This broad program reportedly will include coordination of disarmament as well as defense policies.[41] The all-encompassing nature of the council's mandate seems strikingly similar to that encouraged by the United States in NATO, the concept which France rejected.

French willingness to accept a tighter peacetime commitment and a broader scope in its relationship with Germany than in its relationship with NATO as a whole is a function of lower risk and higher political stakes. In the Franco-German couple the national element is still relatively preserved, while in the wider Alliance it is drowned out by fifteen other voices. Forces under the combined political authority of Paris and Berlin could not act without mutual consent. Integration at this level presents minimal risk to France. One of the main concerns about integration in NATO has always been the fear of being dragged into a war against the interests of the nation (although SACEUR must request member governments' permission to mobilize the forces that would come under his command in crisis or war.)

The political motivation to draw Germany close to the West is strong in the aftermath of unification. France's position of diplomatic influence in post-cold war Europe depends on its ability to balance both the German and Soviet weights on the continent. In approaching this task, Paris faces several major obstacles. First, France must contend with uncertainty as to whether the new Germany will tend toward its former militarism or, at the other extreme, toward neutralist pacifism. Second, and related to the first concern, is the fear that, emboldened by unification, Germany may try to pioneer a more independent course in European security. Finally, France fears being upstaged by Germany in its efforts to win influence with the Soviet Union. The July 1990 summit between Kohl and Gorbachev, during which the latter gave his blessing to German unification, thereby effectively short-stopping the "two plus four" talks between the two Germanies and the four Allied powers, highlighted France's uncertainty as to the future of its special relationship with Moscow.[42] To protect its own diplomatic position France is willing to go farther in its special relationship with Germany than it would in NATO.

The Franco-German couple has been described at times as an "alliance within the Alliance."[43] Yet, while the two security relationships share some common goals and may be mutually supportive, one does not subsume the other. In the French concept of a European security order, bi-national coupling would fulfill a functionally distinct role. General de Gaulle's son, currently a member of the French Senate, described the Franco-German accord as having "completed and partially replaced" the North Atlantic Treaty.[44] That assessment may give the bi-national relationship more credit than it merits, but it does capture the complementary but separate nature of the link between the two levels of security from the French perspective.

The functional distinction between those two levels should become more apparent as stationed forces (especially American) in Europe are reduced. In the report of their June 1990 summit, NATO leaders, with the exception of President Mitterrand, recognized the importance at low force levels of restructuring forces into multi-national units. The French leadership believes that NATO command is not the appropriate framework for such units.[45] At the bilateral level, however, as we have already seen, they take pride in the potential uses for the mixed-manned brigade. At very low force levels, the marginal tactical value of this and similar brigades that might be modeled after it would naturally increase. The brigade will serve as a kind of military laboratory, notes Benoit d'Aboville. It will be "a permanent joint exercise which allows [the French] and the Germans to refine procedures, to know a true interfacing. . . . It is very useful. And it could grow. It could be Europeanized."[46] The model of bilateral military cooperation (if not the brigade per se) could be adopted between France and other partners or along other dyads.

Following the signing of the Elysée Accord, de Gaulle had tried to establish a similar arrangement with Italy, whose president rejected the idea on the grounds that it would be redundant with NATO.[47] Today, as the integrated security structure in Western Europe weakens, a host of opportunities for bilateral relationships similar to the Franco-German coupling may be possible. As noted in France's 1987–1991 military program law, "development [of the relationship with Germany] is a priority. It should be accompanied by an intensification of [French] relations with [its] other European partners, notably with Great Britain."[48] Franco-British cooperation was indeed given a new boost at a May 1990 summit between President Mitterrand and then Prime Minister

Margaret Thatcher. The leaders agreed to joint military exercises in France in 1990, participation of a British battalion in France's Korrigan maneuvers in 1991, and participation of a French helicopter regiment in Britain's September 1992 exercise for reinforcing its armed forces' positions in Germany. They also discussed cooperation in other areas, including nuclear weapons (talk is of a joint long-range, air-to-ground missile) and study of the creation of a common military unit.[49]

Stronger Franco-British coupling could further strengthen France's hand in European security. As the only two nuclear states in a region where nuclear weapons are becoming increasingly unpopular, France and Britain together are more likely to persuade their European partners of the continued value of nuclear deterrence than either of them separately. Moreover, in conjunction with France's special relationship with Germany, a successfully launched special relationship with Great Britain would complete a triangle among the three key players in any future European security order, and this would enhance France's geopolitically privileged position.

The suggestion here is not simply that in the French concept of future European security an elaborate network of bilateral cooperative arrangements would cover the continent. Bi-national structures provide solid institutional frameworks, enabling states to work together while preserving the national element in decision-making. However, alone they will not lead to a united Europe. Although important components of the French vision, bilateral security relationships and, in particular, the Franco-German relationship are not sufficient to fulfill that vision. The ultimate goal in the Gaullist image of Europe is for France to achieve both nationalism and Europeanism. Bilateral security arrangements must therefore be directed toward building the third circle, that of unified Western Europe. Hence, the numerous declarations by Presidents Mitterrand and Kohl professing their commitment to common West European security policy.

In baptizing the joint brigade and Council for Defense and Security in April 1989, the two leaders stressed that their goal was not only to strengthen the bonds between their own countries but also "to cooperate in the emergence of a European identity in matters of defense and security."[50] Throughout 1990 Kohl and Mitterrand were at the vanguard of the movement toward a true West European pillar in European security, trying to impress the example of Franco-German cooperation on their European Community partners. At their summit in April they launched a joint initiative for two intergovernmental conferences of the EC to formulate agenda and structures for economic and monetary union and political and security union respectively. In September they gave further encouragement to that process through a joint declaration which made ample reference to the "unique model of friendly relations and confidence between two states and two neighboring peoples" represented by the Franco-German example.[51] The intergovernmental conferences opened in December, heralded once again by a joint communiqué from Paris and Bonn. This time, the heads of state offered specific proposals for a common West European security agenda, as will be discussed in the next section. Their letter, the product of previous negotiations at the bilateral level, called for "a true common security policy, which would lead ultimately to a common defense."[52] A similar message was conveyed by Foreign Ministers Roland Dumas and Hans Dietrich Genscher in February 1991, at the first ministerial level meeting of the conference on common European foreign policy and defense.[53] In all these documents, France and Germany acknowledge NATO's continued importance, but policy areas which were once NATO's responsibility are now relegated to West European institutions.

WEST EUROPEAN COOPERATION

The concept of a European identity (meaning, in this section, Western European) in security was a dominant theme in French rhetoric in the late 1980s and has been more so since German unification became reality. Then Prime Minister Michel Rocard commented in 1989, "France is actively trying to promote a European sensibility in the area of security, capable of spawning a veritable European strategic culture."[54] Similarly, speaking before the February 1990 *Wehrkunde* conference in Munich, then Defense Minister Chevènement invoked the idea of an "independent European defense" as necessary to "prevent a military vacuum from forming between the two superpowers."[55] References such as these appear to be increasingly common in French statements on defense policy. Even as the current leadership encourages the building of a pan-European confederation joining East and West, it continues to insist that stability in such a confederation will require a western pole of defense.

What precisely the French mean by a common European defense was not sharply defined as of early 1991 but has been coming into focus since initiation of the inter-governmental conference on political union in the European Community. Such a regime would fall somewhere between the extremes of independent national defense and a tightly integrated system, like a resurrected European Defense Community. But along that continuum there is a wide range of alternatives. Institutionally, this third circle might take shape within a revitalized Western European Union joined to the process of political union in the EC.

The role of the WEU, which includes nine of the twelve EC members (Denmark, Greece, and Ireland are not WEU members), has been hotly debated since the start of the inter-governmental conference on political union in December 1990. Its original mandate stressed intra-western arms control and authorized the WEU "to take such steps as may be held to be necessary in the event of a renewal by Germany of a policy of aggression."[56] However, as Germany's accession to the North Atlantic Treaty in 1955 and the stationing of American troops on German soil ensured against the ex-enemy becoming once again an aggressive, independent military power, the WEU faded in importance. For a while, as a forum for discussion of European-wide issues, it served as Great Britain's back door to the EC, a role which it lost when Britain became a Community member in 1973. Then, in 1984, the WEU was revived as a potential institutional basis for a European pillar of defense. Under WEU auspices, European ships coordinated mine-sweeping activities in the Persian Gulf during the Iran-Iraq war, and WEU command conducted naval operations once again in 1990–1991 during the crisis following Iraq's invasion of Kuwait.

In the inter-governmental conference on political union, France has supported the WEU's transformation from "a simple organ of coordination" to "a more effective European alliance." The French leadership would like to see the WEU process eventually incorporated into the political union process of the EC.[57] This contrasts with the opinions of Great Britain and the Netherlands, both of which would prefer the WEU to remain an autonomous body serving as a bridge between NATO and the EC.

While a hybrid of the WEU and EC political union would be the main institution responsible for security at the West European level in the French concept, the European Council, which brings together the heads of state and government of all twelve Community members, would be the executive body charged with setting the policy agenda. France's preference for the European Council has disgruntled, most notably, the European Commission, which is the more supranationally oriented body currently engineering EC unification, and individual Community members such as the Netherlands. Favoring the Council, which makes decisions on the basis of unanimity, over the Commission reflects the importance France will continue to attach to the role of the nation in European security.

In the French vision of common Western European security, the national dimension does not disappear. Hence, the impossibility of a tightly integrated regime. In an interview in February 1990, then Defense Minister Chevènement stressed that the nation must be the "*brique de base*"—the cornerstone—in the construction of a European defense, adding that "for Europe not to slip back into the situation of the inter-war period, when small nations had to choose between two dominations, will depend on [France]."[58] If the West European identity in defense is to become more than a simple "juxtaposition of weaknesses," he repeated in July, "France must take measures to maintain its posture of independent defense."[59]

Independence of defense, as often invoked by French statesmen, means independence of decision-making and not necessarily autonomy of forces. The Gulf war may have proved to be an important object lesson in making this distinction, with relevance for the European security environment. Before the outbreak of war, France's Chief of Armed Forces, General Maurice Schmitt, explained that maintaining national authority over French participation in an international coalition "did not exclude, (on the contrary), cooperation with the military authorities of host countries, first, and with allied forces, second."[60] The clarification through the experience in the Gulf may have helped to untangle the confusion surrounding a major tenet of the Gaullist concept of defense. By demonstrating what is meant in practice by "independence of defense" the war may have made the building of a solid West European defense more tenable among certain political factions in France.

A strong national role hardly rules out coordination of certain tasks that would make common sense at the West European level of security. These would include, for instance, air traffic control and air defense. Chevènement has proposed the creation of multi-national units and ad hoc forces for specific missions, which would be a way of promoting solidarity "parallel to NATO."[61] From the point of view of efficiency at low force levels and establishing the inter-operability needed for joint crisis time intervention, multi-national units would be a logical step.

As noted above, the French leadership considers creation of such units as a task to be undertaken outside the Alliance and opposed the decision of NATO's July 1990 summit meeting to work toward multi-national corps under SACEUR.[62] However, a transformation toward multi-national units could conceivably grow out of experience at the bi-national, Franco-German level of security. We have already seen that the French consider the example of the mixed-manned brigade as a sort of military laboratory that might be Europeanized. This would give substance to the dynamic link between the bi-national and West European levels of security. Policies and practices successfully tested between two nations could be filtered up and adapted for multilateral cooperation. One might also envision that as the delegates to the Franco-German Council for Defense and Security gain some experience and establish "rules of the game," they might find that it would be beneficial to include the other states in their consultations and so try to transform this mechanism into a multi-country forum. West European security would thus become, in part, the constantly evolving product of successes in the circle of two-country relations.

Placed alongside the Atlantic Alliance, security at the level of Western Europe would be both symbiotic and antagonistic, much as we have described the connection between the Alliance and the bi-national level of security. As Jean-Michel Boucheron, Chairman of the Defense Commission of the French National Assembly, aptly explains, "The Western European Union reinforces the cohesion of the Alliance and carries a supplementary guarantee for the realization of the solidarity of its members."[63] That the Atlantic Alliance remain intact and that some U.S. forces remain present in Europe are essential to the French concept of a new European security order, and a more solid, distinctly European defense could continue to support that imperative. However, the Atlantic Alliance must not be allowed to obstruct the emergence of an independent Western European defense, which will be equally important. That the existing trans-Atlantic Alliance and a future Western European defense entity might comfortably exist side-by-side was recognized by NATO foreign ministers at Copenhagen in June 1991. French leaders considered this a major step forward for their concept of security.[64]

As the French foresee a leaner NATO, many of the tasks at the European level of security, guided by a European political authority, would be drawn from what was once NATO's broad agenda. We have already mentioned the example of multi-national units. Another area of common security policy which once came under NATO's auspices but which would now be handled within the new fora of Western Europe is disarmament, arms control, and arms control verification. Addressing the Soviet Voroshilov Military Academy in April 1989, Chevènement pointed out that the WEU, precisely because, unlike NATO, "it does not exercise [military] operational competence and is not, therefore, threatening, can and should play an active role in the disarmament process."[65]

In fact, as its charter and protocols set up a formal apparatus for European arms control, the WEU could be particularly well suited to assume this function in the future. Protocol IV to the Brussels Treaty of 1948 established an Agency for the Control of Armaments, which would be allowed to conduct inspections at irregular intervals (article 11) and would have "free access on demand to plants and depots" (article 12). It also emphasized the requirement of openness on the part of member nations in accounting for armament needs and forces in being, both for NATO missions and for internal defense, (part III, article 13). Protocol II created a mechanism for establishing unanimously agreed-upon ceilings on forces in Western Europe (articles 1 and 5).[66]

While the procedures of the WEU were designed for intra-western arms control, they could be relevant in a future, post–cold war regime. As a set of rules already binding upon nine nations, they could serve as a ready-made framework for more expansive arms control.

Supporting the goals of arms control at the West European level, cooperative mechanisms could be developed for threat assessment and verification. In his February 1990 address before the Institut des hautes études de défense nationale (IHEDN), Foreign Minister Dumas proposed a "regime for information and verification" but did not elaborate on a possible structure.[67] This would represent a clear break with the past, in which the United States, through NATO, essentially dominated intelligence gathering and dissemination.[68]

France would undoubtedly play a critical role in a verification regime. According to one report, the French *Hélios* satellite, scheduled for launch in 1993, will be able to transmit rapidly images with resolution ten times as high as that of France's Spot satellite, currently in orbit, "making France the only country to possess a strategic intelligence capacity independent of the U.S. and the Soviet Union."[69] In addition to possessing its own intelligence-gathering technologies which might benefit its European partners, France, in November 1988, began to head a committee of the Independent European Program Group (IEPG) responsible for developing a list of key sectors for cooperative European development and production. Most of the eleven projects listed, such as satellites, radars, and optics, would be well suited for the task of verification.[70]

In addition to multi-national units, air defense, and arms control and verification, several other functions that might be tested in the Western European circle of a French-shaped security order have been proposed by French statesmen and analysts. Addressing the inter-governmental conference on political union, President Mitterrand and Chancellor Kohl and their respective foreign ministers have offered as possible agenda items: UN peacekeeping measures, nuclear nonproliferation, relations with the U.S.S.R. and countries of Eastern and Central Europe, execution of measures decided on in the Conference on Security and Cooperation in Europe, and relations with countries bordering on the Mediterranean sea.[71] These are all areas in which joint western decisions would have been made, until recently, principally in NATO. However, at NATO's December 1990 foreign ministers meeting, Paris objected, for instance, to NATO's taking the responsibility for expanding East-West diplomatic relations, such that the Atlantic Alliance would become "a sort of CSCE of 22."[72] Henceforth, this dimension of security should be managed at the level of common West European policy, according to France.

François Valentin, former chief of France's armed forces, has tabled the idea of a "joint tactical research" group, which would bring together, at first, France, Great Britain and Germany for discussions "on the use of [military] formations ranging from small units to divisions, on specific matters such as the acquisition and use of intelligence, the exercise of command, ground–air force liaison, etc."[73] In the same spirit, the French government has sponsored a "European session" at the Institut des hautes études de défense nationale, its main officers training institution, which would bring together officers from different European countries.[74]

Pierre Lellouche, foreign policy advisor to conservative leader Jacques Chirac, has proposed creating a European nuclear planning group.[75] Given the importance France would assign to nuclear deterrence in a new security order and the burden of persuading its partners of the value of the *force de frappe* as an effective Euro-deterrent, establishing such an organ would be a wise initiative. A Western European NPG could be the meeting ground for French and British nuclear cooperation. Like NATO's NPG, this body could serve as a forum for consultation on targeting, command and control, etcetera.

Finally, the common West European pole of security would serve the important function of working toward construction of the "fourth circle" in the French vision of European security—the European confederation, bringing East and West together in a cooperative pan-European security system. Chevènement alluded to such a role in addressing the WEU in December 1989, reminding the members of that body that "in the new [historical] period, the countries of Western Europe are called on to play the principal role in assuring a constant dialogue with their Eastern European brothers."[76] Just as bilateral security arrangements must contribute to the creation of an independent Western European level of security, according to the French concept, so a united Western Europe should be the engine driving a broader confederation.

PAN-EUROPEAN CONFEDERATION

Like the concept of a common Western European defense, the goal of a pan-European confederation has been much invoked by France's political leadership but only loosely defined. Foreign Minister Dumas, for instance, described confederation as "the most flexible form of association between countries that want to come together on what is most important."[77] The emphasis on flexibility precludes articulation of any preconceived institutional notion which might constrain the confederation before it is built.

One feature which would characterize this fourth overlapping circle, as it would the other three, is the importance of the nation as the basic unit. Like NATO, the Franco-German and other bilateral relationships, and Western European defense, a pan-European confederation could not be so integrated as to suppress national identity and national, autonomous decision-making. Thus Dumas has explained that the broadest level of European security "is a matter of a collective structure, in the sense that thirty-five countries historically play an integral part in the European strategic equilibrium, *collective but respecting the national dimension of each one's engagement*" (my emphasis).[78] Then Defense Minister Chevènement too observed, "We cannot content ourselves with a Europe of the Twelve," adding further, "Europe cannot be just a technocratic super-state, but a confederation of free and democratic nations."[79] As in building a Western European identity in defense, the strength of the nation would be both the driving force behind confederation and its limiting factor.

Promoting the importance of the nation as the fundamental unit in Europe as a whole, France has been the prime exponent of the view that pan-European arms control should fall within the framework not of the old two-bloc system, but rather of the Conference on Security and Cooperation in Europe. In the deliberations to prepare for the first round of Conventional Forces in Europe negotiations, France insisted on coupling CFE to upcoming talks in the CSCE (which happened to be on human rights), so that conventional arms control would be formally associated with that format. The United States opposed this initiative, maintaining that CFE should be a separate and autonomous process. The compromise ultimately reached was that CFE would be "within the framework of the CSCE process, but autonomous as to participation, procedures and certain other modalities."[80] The only participants in the first round of CFE were country members of either NATO or the Warsaw Pact. However, the final treaty, signed at the Paris summit of CSCE heads of state and government in November 1990, and accompanying documents refer only to countries, never mentioning either of the alliances by name. While this may seem to be a technicality, the French take the distinction quite seriously, and in public remarks, French leaders constantly remind their audiences that the current framework for conventional arms control is the product of French initiative.[81]

However, the French are sensitive to the fact that revolutionary changes in Europe since CFE began have rendered the current process, paradoxically, an obstacle to rather than a motor for more rapid, comprehensive change. They realize that despite French efforts, CFE became associated in public perception with the two blocs. At a time when blocs are dissolving, CFE froze the *status quo*. Therefore, Dumas observed in February 1990, the current political environment "justifies a more complete approach [to future arms control], which would further incorporate the different aspects of security and not resume a simple proportional reduction of armaments limited by treaty." He also proposed that in the next round of negotiations the forum of 22 should be expanded to include all 35 CSCE nations (now 38, since the three Baltic republics were admitted).[82] That recommendation echoed Defense Minister Chevènement's proposal a few days earlier that the next round must extend beyond the Atlantic-to-the-Urals region, encompassing instead the area "from San Francisco to Vladivostok, because Europe must not become a 'field of particular restrictions' under superpower management."[83]

In a small revolt against convention, in December 1989, during the pan-European talks on Confidence and Security Building Measures (CSBM), France advanced a proposal with Hungary on ways "to intensify East-West military contacts . . . to reinforce the role of foreign military attachés and to expand their freedom of movement." This was the first instance of members of two different alliances co-sponsoring a formal resolution.[84] While marginal in its particular impact, this incident illustrates the type of cooperation France would envision at the pan-European level of security. National autonomy of action would be preserved, and the notions of West and East would not restrict possible cooperation among combinations of countries within the confederation. France's privileged position in leading this type of cooperation is evident from its political ties with Eastern Europe. As Jolyon Howorth observes, "France has more direct lines of communication . . . with the nations and peoples of Eastern Europe than any other European country."[85] In an address to the nation in July 1990, President Mitterrand drew attention to the efforts of French diplomacy since 1985 to establish stronger ties with those countries. He has made official visits to all the states of Eastern and Central Europe and boasts friendly relations with most of their leaders.[86]

A final observation should be noted on the relation between the French idea of a European confederation and the Conference on Security and Cooperation in Europe. On the one hand, France considers CSCE an important forum, especially for arms control, in that it transcends a bloc mentality in pan-European consultations. On the other hand, the French emphasize, the CSCE process must not be confused with the end product. The CSCE is not the proverbial concert of Europe. It is simply a way of getting to that goal. As Foreign Minister Dumas explained, "From [the French] point of view we don't see the confederation as the means of resolving the questions of security in Europe. Rather, it will be the result of the solutions we will have found in response to those questions. Its advent will be, precisely, the symbol of our success in surmounting the problems that still exist."[87]

In the final analysis, the definition of European confederation will only be known once it is achieved. To characterize it in advance would be to restrict its potential. This final overlapping circle is the least definable of the four, but in the French vision of European security it is as critical as the other three.

THE CONTINUED RELEVANCE OF
NUCLEAR DETERRENCE

Thus far we have established that a French-shaped European security order would favor cooperative over integrative structures and that it would be multi-dimensional, attaching equal importance to four distinct but mutually supportive levels of security. This discussion has emphasized that at all levels the French influence would try to achieve maximum cooperation while preserving national identity and autonomy. That theme is vividly reflected in the French concept of the future role of nuclear deterrence. According to the French vision, the importance of nuclear deterrence would grow pursuant to reduced conventional force levels, and France's own *force de frappe* would become a centerpiece of European security. French-controlled, it would be a constant affirmation of France's identity and autonomy; yet, nominally dedicated to Community-wide deterrence, it would be, in the French view, a catalyst for West European unity.

In his report on the 1990–1993 military program law, Chairman of the Defense Commission of the National Assembly Jean-Michel Boucheron noted that dissent in Europe over the future of flexible response strategy, accelerated by the debate over modernization of NATO's short-range nuclear weapons, signaled a "return to deterrence," as exemplified by France's nuclear force and nuclear strategy. He wrote, "The only strategic concept common to all the countries of Europe on which European security can be based is that of nuclear deterrence. . . . The *force de frappe* of our country can be, in effect, the rallying point to the principle of deterrence for our European allies and already represents one of the bases of European identity in the area of defense."[88] That the French can see in the new security environment a return to true deterrence while others, as described in chapter two, might see a return to true flexible response highlights the ambiguities of doctrine.

From the French point of view, the two distinguishing features which will make the French nuclear deterrent credible as a European deterrent in a future regime are the doctrine of sufficiency and the "final warning" mission of France's tactical (prestrategic) nuclear weapons.

The French believe that together these two characteristics of the *force de frappe* embrace a policy of pure deterrence, in contrast to what they perceive as the war-fighting concept inherent in NATO's short-range nuclear weapons and flexible response strategy. Foreign Minister Dumas addressed this difference between French and NATO nuclear concepts in his remarks before the IHEDN in February 1990, observing that "the concept of sufficiency, which underlies [France's] policy of deterrence, remains adapted to the [foreseeable] circumstances."[89] In other words, because of commitment to "sufficiency," France, unlike NATO, is not in danger of its nuclear arsenal being perceived as anything but a pure deterrent.

Strengthening this idea, the French claim, is their refusal to use nuclear weapons in a battlefield mode. As President Mitterrand articulated this policy in October 1988, "Prestrategic weapons are not intended as an extension of conventional weapons. They are used by definition at the start of the nuclear process."[90] The firing of a *Pluton* missile (to be replaced by *Hadès* in 1992) or a medium-range air-launched missile (ASMP—*air-sol moyenne portée*) would be a clear signal (*l'ultime avertissement*) to an aggressor of French intent to launch strategic nuclear weapons if hostilities did not cease. According to French doctrine, prestrategic nuclear weapons would not be used for any other purpose.

The pure deterrent role of their nuclear weapons, the French maintain, renders them an eminently stabilizing factor in European security. To support this point of view they cite Soviet statements of relative tolerance of the *force de frappe*. For example, returning from a tour of the Soviet Union in April 1989, Defense Minister Chevènement announced, "Moscow seems to accept the existence of a difference in operational concept between France, which would resort to [nuclear] weapons only to deliver 'the final warning' to an adversary threatening its 'vital interests,' and NATO, which would use these weapons in a tactical mode, within the strategy of 'flexible response,' thereby accepting the risk of a nuclear battle in Europe." He added that a spokesman for the Soviet defense establishment, General Lebediev, had affirmed, "[The Soviet Union] will not question the French *Hadès* missile."[91] Presumably this means the Soviets would not insist that by deploying *Hadès* France, although not a signatory to the Intermediate-range Nuclear Forces (INF) Treaty, would somehow be violating the spirit of good faith between East and West which resulted from that treaty.

Boucheron noted that General Moïseev, the chief of staff of the Soviet armed forces, also stated (July 1989) that the Soviet Union considers the *force de frappe* and French strategy less destabilizing than flexible response.[92]

France continued to distinguish its idea of pure deterrence from NATO's nuclear employment doctrine even following the Alliance's modification of its doctrine at the July 1990 summit. The report of that meeting concluded that nuclear weapons would henceforth be considered "truly weapons of last resort." President Mitterrand objected to this decision on the grounds that any doctrine which envisions a hierarchical scale of firepower, from conventional artillery to nuclear weapons, implies that war in Europe is still thinkable. Declaring nuclear weapons to be weapons of last resort leaves a window of opportunity to a potential aggressor in search of limited territorial gains (e.g., the infamous "Hamburg grab," once hypothesized by western analysts). He considered the change in doctrine only marginal and still diametrically opposed to the French doctrine. "If everyone knows that everything is at stake from the point of departure," Mitterrand stated after the July 1990 NATO summit, "then there will be no war."[93]

The non-threatening nature of the *force de frappe*, Chevènement has argued, will support the goals of conventional arms control in Europe, as "nuclear deterrence will guarantee the stability of the conventional equilibrium at the low level we are seeking."[94] The existence of a stable deterrent, the French envision, will encourage further conventional reductions and will guarantee the peace long after those reductions. For this reason, France has protected ongoing development of new nuclear systems, including the dual-capable (i.e., capable of carrying both conventional and nuclear payload) *Mirage 2000 N* bomber and the *Hadès* prestrategic missile. Furthermore, it has adamantly defended the inviolability of its "sufficient" nuclear force in current or future rounds of arms control. At the NATO heads of state meeting in May 1989, President Mitterrand announced emphatically, "French air forces which would be useable for the autonomous deterrent strategy cannot be included at any stage in negotiations."[95] France refuses to withdraw any systems that might detract from its deterrent capability. Willingness to do so would reflect either an acknowledgment that in fact the *force de frappe* had been more than sufficient or inconsistency within the French leadership.

Similarly, the French leadership has voiced its strong objections to any external phenomena that might compromise France's autonomous nuclear deterrence, such as ballistic missile defense (BMD) systems and tactics of conventional deterrence. In his report on France's military program law for 1990–1993, Defense Commission Chairman Boucheron opened with a detailed critique of the American Strategic Defense Initiative, which he condemned as antithetical to deterrence.[96] That SDI was the first topic of discussion in a 758-page report seemed to indicate a disproportionate level of French concern over a concept which lost most of its steam in the United States following the end of the Reagan administration. Furthermore, the real source of French fear was never an American SDI per se, but rather, the possibility of an American-Soviet race to deploy ballistic missile defenses, which would render the *force de frappe* considerably less effective. In the early 1990s, the likelihood that the Soviet Union could actually afford the expense of competing with the United States in developing a BMD when it can barely hold together its own domestic economy is extremely remote. The strong French perception, indicated in Boucheron's report, that SDI still poses a real threat to deterrence reflects how intensely protective the French are of the *force de frappe*.

Perhaps a more legitimate French concern is the possibility of conventional deterrence gaining favor over nuclear deterrence in European governments. The concept of conventional deterrence is based on the goal of raising the nuclear threshold by improving conventional capability, most likely through high technology weapons and target acquisition systems, to the point where it can theoretically substitute for nuclear capability. The French believe that conventional deterrence actually undermines true deterrence by increasing a potential aggressor's confidence in his ability to risk attack without fear of nuclear retaliation. True deterrence, they maintain, requires a low nuclear threshold to assure a potential aggressor that any attack would provoke a nuclear response. Boucheron wrote, "Deterrence is properly the domain of nuclear weapons: whatever the performance of conventional arms, they cannot assure by themselves a decisive advantage over the adversary. . . . The notion of conventional deterrence," he concluded, "is illusory, destabilizing and dangerous."[97] Defending his report before the National Assembly, Boucheron stressed that canceling any of France's major nuclear programs would be the equivalent of admitting the acceptability of conventional deterrence in Europe.[98] Former Defense Minister Chevènement has similarly warned against raising the nuclear threshold "to the point where deterrence itself would come to lose all meaning."[99] For deterrence to be accepted as the future strategic doctrine for Europe overall, the French believe, France's commitment to this idea must serve as a consistent model.

Concern for maintaining a consistent level of deterrence has led to debate in France over how to modernize the *force de frappe* for the Twenty-first Century. Around the year 2000 the eighteen S3 land-based missiles on the *plateau d'Albion* will have reached the end of their life cycle. One school of thought favors abandoning the plateau at that time and replacing the S3s with a long-range (between 600 and 1000 km, depending on altitude) air-launched missile. That system might be developed jointly with the British and could be promoted as a "Euro-deterrent." A second school of thought, supported by former Defense Minister André Giraud, amongst others, considers a new generation air-launched missile to be useful, but too vulnerable by itself. They recommend that it be developed alongside a new land-based mobile missile, the S45.[100] A triad consisting of modernized sea-launched and ground-launched missiles, as well as a new long-range air-launched missile was proposed to the National Assembly in June 1991 by an advisor to Defense Minister Pierre Joxe. The advisor suggested that, in the interests of common European security, the air-launched component might be based "on the territory of another European state."[101] The issue of how France should fulfill its security obligations is becoming increasingly divisive and may impede France from taking a leading role in European security, as will be discussed in the next chapter.

In a French-shaped European security order a constant, stable level of "sufficient" nuclear deterrence would not necessarily have to justify itself in response to a particular threat. As argued in chapter two, concern in Europe about the uncertain and potentially unstable nature of the international system sustains the high premium Europeans attach to a stable, non-aggressive military force, even in the current political environment. From the French point of view, this is also the *raison d'être* for a permanent nuclear deterrent. In that sense, the *force de frappe* is a long-term watchdog at the service of continental peace.

However, until Europe fully accepts the value of a standing nuclear force absent a clear enemy, it will be useful for French leaders to continue to justify improvement of the *force de frappe* vis-à-vis the Soviet nuclear threat. Thus political leaders, such as conservative. (Rassemblement Pour la République—RPR) party leader and former

Prime Minister Jacques Chirac, press for a continued effort to strengthen the *force de frappe* by arguing that "even in the event of a disarmament agreement in Europe, the U.S.S.R. would remain, *de facto*, the dominant military power on our continent, and nuclear deterrence would remain, for France as well as Europe, the condition for a relationship with Moscow in political equilibrium."[102] Then Defense Minister Chevènement responded similarly to questions about the rationale for continuing to build the *Hadès* missile, the range of which would be about 480 km, now that the Warsaw Pact military threat has disappeared. In an interview in *Der Spiegel* in March 1990, he commented, "The concern that Germans frequently express regarding the several tens of French [nuclear] weapons, while there are some 1800 Soviet weapons acknowledged by the Soviets themselves, always surprises me."[103] In addition to being a more concrete, rather than a philosophical justification, citing the continued presence of Soviet nuclear weapons hides the fact that France may, perhaps, also see the *force de frappe* as a check against Germany's own military aspirations.

In the long term, for France to succeed in making the *force de frappe* the centerpiece of a European security order, its neighbors would have to fully accept the permanent value of deterrence as independent of any particular, momentary threat to the peace. They would also have to be convinced that France's vital interests are so closely linked to their own, by virtue of geography and by virtue of the emergence of a united, cooperative European security system, that a nationally controlled nuclear deterrent would be almost indistinguishable, with respect to the ends it would serve in peace or war, from a multi-laterally controlled deterrent. Ultimately, as Gaullism emphasizes, there will always be a limit to how closely the vital interests of one nation can be identified with the vital interests of others. Therefore, the Europeanization of the French nuclear force would never be absolute. The goal for France is to approach the ideal as closely as possible without sacrificing national autonomy over nuclear decision-making.

This dilemma echoes the unresolved MLF–*force de frappe* debate of the 1960s. Then as now, the challenge before France was to reconcile national with cooperative, supranational dimensions of security. Today France is in a seemingly paradoxical situation where, it hopes, creating a unified Western Europe will magnify its particular national role by enhancing the credibility of declarations that the *force de frappe* is a truly European deterrent.

force de frappe

Success in this task will rely fundamentally on European acceptance of the French concept of deterrence. As Chevènement noted, a flexible component of the *force de frappe*, such as the *Mirage 2000* bomber deployed with medium-range missiles, can advance the goal of European deterrence, but ultimately "the existence of a weapon cannot substitute for the political will of Europeans themselves."[104] According to some observers, this will may in fact be evolving. Boucheron asserts that French doctrine has already had an undeniable influence in shaping the new Europe. The key to that impact, he believes, is that "deterrence has regained legitimacy with [France's] allies."[105] In the same spirit, Pierre Lellouche finds that "Germans now have a greater understanding of the importance of the French deterrent to European deterrence as a whole."[106] In June 1989, the newly appointed Belgian minister of foreign affairs announced that "the European NATO countries would no longer need nuclear weapons if Great Britain and France were to place them under the protection of their nuclear deterrents."[107]

Thus, as the French would like to believe, a "return" to deterrence may grow out of the new security environment in Europe. The critical test for France will be whether it can solidify this trend without Europe slipping from cooperative into integrative security. It may be that, from the point of view of France's neighbors, a French nuclear force can provide a truly European deterrent only when European security is tightly integrated. If this is true, then instead of a trump card, the *force de frappe* could become France's Achilles heel.

The French would have to contend with two potentially conflicting imperatives. On the one hand, a French nuclear deterrent must be at the center of a new European security order, which might require extensive integration in Europe. On the other hand, the new order must favor loose cooperation over integration, in order to preserve national decision-making autonomy in all respects. Trying to reconcile these two goals could actually paralyze French initiative. If French leaders press for a central role for the *force de frappe* as a European deterrent, the rest of Europe may require tight integration of security as a necessary *quid pro quo*. If French leaders insist on loosely cooperative structures of security, the rest of Europe may be less accepting of the *force de frappe* as a permanent fixture, demanding that France put its nuclear forces on the arms control table. The latter alternative would put France in a very uncomfortable position, which could lead to its inadvertent political self-isolation in Europe. Either scenario could develop into a real crisis within France.

NOTES

1. Interview in late February 1990. [This information was provided on a non-attribution basis.] Information provided by this officer has been extremely helpful to the writing of the current work. He is referred to in the text as "a high-ranking American officer, formerly serving at SHAPE."

2. References to France's national "rank" allude to the central chapter of de Gaulle's *Mémoires de guerre*. Paris: Plon, 1954, 1956, 1959. (Printed in three volumes.)

3. Pierre Lellouche, "Paris: deux logiques pour une stratégie," *Le Point* (7 March 1988), p. 39.

4. François Mitterrand, *Réflexions sur la politique extérieure de la France* (Paris, Fayard, 1986), pp. 11, 20, 98, 100–101.

5. "France is my fatherland, Europe is my future." Cited in John G. Mason, "Mitterrand, the Socialists, and French Nuclear Policy," in Philippe G. Le Prestre, ed., *French Security Policy in a Disarming World* (Boulder, CO, Lynne Rienner Publishers, 1989), p. 76.

6. Jean-Paul Pigasse, "La CED enfin!" *Le Monde*, 3 March 1990, p. 2. For a rebuttal, see, Maurice Delarue, "Réponse à Jean-Paul Pigasse," *Le Monde*, 21 March 1990, p. 2.

7. U.S. Department of State, *American Foreign Policy, 1950–1955, Vol. I* (Washington, DC, GPO, 1957), "Treaty of the European Defense Community," 27 May 1952, pp. 1107–1150.

8. Alfred Grosser, "German Question, French Anxiety," *The New York Times*, 26 December 1989, p. A27.

9. Joseph Rovan, "L'heure des deux unités," *Le Monde*, 2 March 1990, p. 2.

10. Jean-Pierre Chevènement, "La France et la sécurité de l'Europe," *Politique Étrangère* (no. 3, 1990), p. 528.

11. Roland Dumas, *Discours du ministre d'état à l'IHEDN, le 6 février 1990*, Bulletin d'Information, Diplo Paris, 7 February 1990, p. 9.

12. Cited in Jérôme Dumoulin and Sylvie Pierre-Brossolette, "Chevènement: la réunification n'est pas d'actualité," *L'Express* (24 November 1989), p. 30.

13. James A. Baker III, *A New Europe, a New Atlanticism: Architecture for a New Era*, Address to the Berlin Press Club at the Steigenberger Hotel, Berlin, 12 December 1989, Current Policy, 1233, (Washington, DC, U.S. Department of State, Bureau of Public Affairs, 1989).

14. Jacques Amalric, "Les propositions de M. James Baker sur l'Europe suscitent à Paris satisfaction et perplexité," *Le Monde*, 15 December 1989, p. 3.

15. Cited in Claire Tréan, "Paris et Washington réduisent leurs divergences sur la défense," *Le Monde*, 8 June 1991, p. 8.

16. Cited in Werner J. Feld, "International Implications of the Joint Franco-German Brigade," *Military Review* (February 1990), p. 8.

17. Feld, p. 4.

18. Yves Cuau, "Les français, doivent-ils avoir peur de l'Allemagne?" *L'Express* (16 March 1990), p. 40.

19. Claire Tréan, "Les modalités de la réunification de l'Allemagne détermineront l'avenir de l'OTAN," *Le Monde*, 6 February 1990.

20. Henri De Bresson, " 'Il y a des moments où le silence est lourd d'ambiguités,' affirme M. Roland Dumas à Berlin-Ouest," *Le Monde*, 6 March 1990, p. 6.

21. Roland Dumas, "One Germany—If Europe Agrees," *The New York Times*, 13 March 1990, p. A29.

22. "L'intervention télévisée du Président de la République," *Le Monde*, 17 July 1990, p. 6.

23. Claire Tréan, "Pour MM. Kohl et Mitterrand, le rattachement de la RDA devra renforcer le couple franco-allemand," *Le Monde*, 20 September 1990, p. 4.

24. "M. Chevènement: 'On ne peut pas se contenter d'une Europe à Douze'," AGRA 1/1901, 3 January 1990. [NB: AGRA and AFP in citations refer to French news wire services.]

25. Cited in Tréan, "Paris et Washington réduisent leurs divergences sur la défense," p. 8.

26. Tréan, "Paris et Washington réduisent leurs divergences sur la défense," p. 8.

27. "M. Giscard d'Estaing souhaite 'une solidarité' franco-allemande en matière de défense," *Le Monde*, 3 April 1990, p. 3.

28. André Giraud, "Construction européene et défense," *Politique Étrangère* (no. 3, 1990), p. 519.

29. François Valentin, "Quelle défense pour quelle Europe?" *Politique Étrangère* (no. 3, 1990), pp. 536, 540.

30. Frédéric Bozo, "La France et l'OTAN: vers une nouvelle alliance," *Défense Nationale* (January 1991), p. 28.

31. Interview with Benoit d'Aboville, French Consulate, New York, NY, 8 January 1990.

32. Claire Tréan, "L'OTAN reconnaît à l'Europe des Douze le droit de se doter d'une politique de sécurité," *Le Monde*, 10 June 1991, p. 3.

33. "Excerpts from Treaty between the French Republic and the FRG on Franco-German cooperation," January 1963, reprinted in Robbin F. Laird, ed., *Strangers and Friends: The Franco-German Security Relationship* (London, Pinter Publishers, 1989), Appendix B, p. 141.

34. See Appendices C and D in Laird, ed., *Strangers and Friends*.

35. Cited in Feld, p. 6.

36. "FAR from Perfect," *The Economist* (26 September 1987), p. 63.

37. "La brigade franco-allemande a une valeur militaire réduite," *Le Monde*, 22 April 1989, p. 6. See also "France Weighing Value of Political Autonomy against Trend toward Defense Cooperation," *Aviation Week and Space Technology* (12 October 1987), p. 132.

38. Cited in "M. Chevènement plaide pour un système de sécurité collective en Europe," *Le Monde*, 5 June 1990, p. 7.

39. See Ian Gambles, *Prospects for West European Security Co-operation*, Adelphi Paper, 244 (London, The International Institute for Strategic Studies, 1989), p. 49.

40. "MM. François Mitterrand et Helmut Kohl ont présidé la première réunion du conseil de défense et de sécurité," *Le Monde*, 22 April 1989, p. 6.

41. "Paris et Bonn souhaitent intensifier leur coopération en matière de défense et de désarmement," AFP, 20 April 1989.

42. David S. Yost, "France in the New Europe," *Foreign Affairs* (Winter 1990/91), pp. 114–15.

43. Robert Grant, "French Security Policy and the Franco-German Relationship," in Laird, ed., *Strangers and Friends*, p. 21.

44. Sénat de la République Française, *Avis présenté au nom de la commission des affaires étrangères, de la défense, et des forces armées, sur le projet de loi de finances pour 1990 considéré comme adopté par l'Assemblée Nationale aux termes de l'article 49, alinéa 3, de la Constitution*, Tome VI, Défense, Section forces terrestres, No. 62, Opinion prepared by Philippe de Gaulle, 9e Leg., le sess., 21 November 1989, p. 10.

45. Yost, p. 119.

46. d'Aboville, interview (see this chapter, note 31).

47. Richard Helms, Deputy Director for Plans, Central Intelligence Agency, *Views of President Charles de Gaulle regarding the United States, Europe and NATO; and Italian Reaction*, Memorandum to Director of Central Intelligence (18 March 1964). Found in National Security Archive, Nuclear History Collection. NB: All historical documents used in this study are available at the National Security Archive, 1755 Massachusetts Ave., NW, Suite 500, Washington, DC 20036. This will be indicated henceforth as "NSA."

48. Cited in Yves Boyer and John Roper, "Conclusion," in Yves Boyer, Pierre Lellouche, and John Roper, eds., *Franco-British Defence Cooperation* (London, Royal Institute of International Affairs, 1988), pp. 182–83.

49. Dominique Dhombres, "Paris et Londres vont renforcer leur coopération en matière de défense," *Le Monde*, 7 May 1990, p. 4. See also "Ménage à deux," *The Economist* (24 March 1990), p. 29.

50. "Paris et Bonn souhaitent intensifier leur coopération en matière de défense et de désarmement."

51. "La déclaration commune [de MM. Kohl et Mitterrand]," *Le Monde*, 20 September 1990, p. 4.

52. "La lettre commune de MM. Kohl et Mitterrand," *Le Monde*, 10 December 1990, p. 4. See also Claire Tréan, "MM. Kohl et Mitterrand relancent en commun la dynamique européenne," *Le Monde*, 10 December 1990, pp. 1, 4.

53. Philippe Lemaître, "La France et l'Allemagne relancent le projet de politique étrangère et de défense européennes communes," *Le Monde*, 6 February 1991, p. 28.

54. Cited in Assemblée Nationale de la République Française, *Rapport fait au nom de la commission de la défense nationale et des forces armées sur le projet de loi de programmation (no. 733) relatif à l'équipement militaire pour les années 1990–1993*, No. 897, Report prepared by Jean-Michel Boucheron, 9e Leg., le sess., 2 October 1989, p. 91. [Hereafter cited as Boucheron, *Rapport*.]

55. "La France en faveur d'une défense Européene indépendante," AFP, 4 February 1990. See also Jean-Pierre Chevènement, "La France et la sécurité de l'Europe," *Politique Étrangère* (no. 3, 1990), p. 527.

56. U.S. Department of State, *American Foreign Policy, 1950–1955, Vol. I*, "Articles of the Western European Union," p. 968. See also Chapter 1, note 4.

57. Lemaître p. 28.

58. "Paix et équilibre," *Armées d'Aujourd'hui* (February 1990), p. 8.

59. Jacques Isnard, "*Un entretien avec M. Chevènement*," *Le Monde*, 13 July 1990, p. 9.

60. "Le général Schmitt affirme qu'il ne faut pas confondre 'autonomie des forces' et 'autonomie de décision'," *Le Monde*, 21 November 1990, p. 4.

61. Chevènement, "LaFrance et la sécurité de l'Europe," pp. 528–29.

62. Yost, p. 119.

63. Boucheron, *Rapport*, p. 89. The symbiosis between NATO and the WEU is in fact recognized in the 1954 protocols to the WEU Brussels Treaty of 1948. Article III of Protocol I, for example, affirms cooperation with NATO and reliance "on the appropriate Military Authorities of NATO for information and advice on military matters." U.S. Department of State, *American Foreign Policy, 1950–1955, Vol. 1*, "Protocol No. 1 (and annex) Modifying and Completing the Brussels Treaty," 23 October 1954, p. 973.

64. Tréan, "L'OTAN reconnaît à l'Europe des Douze le droit de se doter d'une politique de sécurité," p. 3.

65. Cited in Boucheron, *Rapport*, p. 90.

66. U.S. Department of State, *American Foreign Policy, 1950–1955, Vol. I*, "Protocol II of the Western European Union and Protocol IV on the Agency

of Western European Union for the Control of Armaments," 23 October 1954, pp. 977, 978, 984, 986, 987.

67. Dumas, *Discours du ministre d'état à l'IHEDN, le 6 février 1990*, p. 3.

68. See Introduction, note 35.

69. Assemblée Nationale de la République Française, *Rapport fait au nom de la commission de la défense nationale et des forces armées sur le projet de loi de programmation (no. 432) relatif à l'équipement militaire pour les années 1987–1991*, No. 622, Report prepared by François Fillon, 8e Leg., 2e sess., 7 April 1987, p. 101.

Citing the expected capacity of the *Hélios*, as well as France's *Syracuse* communications satellite, Pierre Esteve, a deputy of the National Assembly, proposed the concept of a European Satellite Agency, which could govern treaty verification and crisis management. See Pierre Esteve in Assemblée Nationale de la République Française, "Équipement militaire pour les années 1990–1993," Débats Parlementaires, *Journal officiel de la république française*, 9e Leg., le sess., 4e séance, 4 October 1989, p. 3082.

70. Boucheron, *Rapport*, p. 87.

71. "La lettre commune de MM. Kohl et Mitterrand," *Le Monde*, p. 4, and Lemaître, p. 28.

72. Jean de la Guérivière, "Le renforcement des compétences de l'OTAN et le rôle des Européens restent controversés," *Le Monde*, 20 December 1990, p. 28.

73. François Valentin, "Co-operation between Conventional Forces in Europe: A French View," in Boyer, Lellouche, and Roper, eds., *Franco-British Defence Cooperation*, p. 65.

74. Cited in Boucheron, *Rapport*, p. 91.

75. Pierre Lellouche, "Rebuild or Decay: The Future of the European Security System (A French Perspective)," in Stanley R. Sloan, ed., *NATO in the 1990s* (Washington, DC, Pergamon-Brassey's, 1989), p. 260. More recently, conservative leader Jacques Chirac proposed putting some prestrategic weapons from France's and Britain's respective arsenals at Europe's common disposal. He also called for creation of a defense council at the level of heads of state and government of Western Europe. See "M. Chirac favorable à des unités multinationales sous commandement européen," *Le Monde*, 25 May 1990, p. 7.

76. Jean-Pierre Chevènement, *Discours du ministre de la défense devant l'assemblée de l'U.E.O., le 5 décembre 1989*, Bulletin d'Information, 7 December 1989.

Similarly, Lellouche writes, "In the long term, only the establishment of an axis of economic and political power in Western Europe that is capable of insuring its own defense can provide the framework for possible reunification of the two parts of mainland Europe." Lellouche, in Sloan, ed., p. 254.

77. Dumas, "One Germany—If Europe Agrees," p. A29.

78. Dumas, *Discours du ministre d'état à l'IHEDN, le 6 février 1989*, p. 3.

79. "M. Chevènement: 'On ne peut pas se contenter d'une Europe à Douze,' " AGRA 1/1901, 3 January 1990.

80. Serge Schmemann, "The Tangle Thickens in Two Sets of East-West Talks," *The New York Times*, 29 November 1988, p. A8.

81. See, for example, Jean-Pierre Chevènement, *Allocution du ministre de la défense devant le centre des hautes études de l'armement, le 12 septembre 1989*, Diplo Paris, 21 September 1989, p. 8.

See also Claire Tréan, "MM. Dumas, Genscher et De Michelis prônent une accélération du processus de désarmement conventionnel," *Le Monde*, 27 January 1990, p. 4.

82. Dumas, *Discours du ministre d'état à l'IHEDN, le 6 février 1990*, pp. 4–5.

83. "Un accord à Vienne sur le désarmement n'apportera pas de changement à l'équipement des forces françaises," *Le Monde*, 2 February 1990, p. 3.

84. "La France va créer un corps d'inspecteurs du désarmement," *Le Monde*, 13 January 1990, p. 10.

85. Jolyon Howorth, "Consensus and Mythology: Security Alternatives in Post-Gaullist France," in Robert Aldrich and John Connell, eds., *France in World Politics* (London, Routledge, 1989), p. 30.

86. "L'intervention télévisée du président de la République," p. 6.

87. Dumas, *Discours du ministre d'état à l'IHEDN, le 6 février 1990*, p. 7.

88. Boucheron, *Rapport*, pp. 76, 82–83.

89. Dumas, *Discours du ministre d'état à l'IHEDN, le 6 février 1990*, p. 6.

90. Cited in Boucheron, *Rapport*, p. 238.

91. "M. Chevènement en URSS: Première visite d'un ministre français de la défense depuis 12 ans," AGRA, 2 April 1989.

92. Cited in Boucheron, *Rapport*, p. 82.

93. " 'La logique voudra que l'armée française stationée en Allemagne regagne son pays,' déclare M. Mitterrand," *Le Monde*, 9 July 1990, p. 5.

94. Chevènement, *Allocution du ministre de la défense, le 12 septembre 1989*, p. 14. See also Dumoulin and Pierre-Brossolette, p. 30.

95. Cited in Claire Tréan, "Les Occidentaux acceptent de négocier sur les armes nucléaires à courte portée mais refusent leur élimination totale," *Le Monde*, 31 May 1989, p. 7.

96. Boucheron, *Rapport*, pp. 16–20.

97. Boucheron, *Rapport*, pp. 29, 30.

98. Jean-Michel Boucheron in Assemblée Nationale de la République Française, "Équipement militaire pour les années 1990–1993," le séance, 3 October 1989, p. 3024.

99. Isnard, "Un entretien avec M. Chevènement," p. 9.

100. Andrée Giraud, "Nos armes nucléaires," *Le Monde*, 16 January 1991, p. 2. See also Jacques Isnard, "M. Mitterrand devrait choisir entre un missile mobile et un système d'arme nucléaire adapté à l'avion Rafale," *Le Monde*, 16 January 1991, p. 16.

101. Cited in Jacques Isnard, "Un conseiller de M. Joxe plaide pour le maintien de la 'triade' nucléaires," *Le Monde*, 19 June 1991, p. 12. Isnard,

102. Jacques Chirac, "Une remise en cause insidieuse de notre défense," *Le Monde*, 10 June 1989, p. 1.

103. Cited in "M. Chevènement: 'le missile Hadès peut être utile à l'Europe entière,' " *Le Monde*, 13 March 1990, p. 6.

104. Cited in Jacques Isnard, "La France, promesse d'une Europe de la défense," *Le Monde*, 14 July 1988, p. 11.

105. Boucheron, *Rapport*, p. 8.

106. Lellouche, "Rebuild or Decay," in Sloan, ed., p. 256.

107. "M. Eyskens pour une Europe sous garantie militaire franco-britannique," AFP, 20 June 1989.

CHAPTER 4

THE GAULLIST LEGACY:
HELP OR HINDRANCE TO A NEW FRENCH
ROLE IN EUROPEAN SECURITY?

The future of Europe which has been described up to this point would seem to be very favorable to France. A historic opportunity exists to alter the shape of security on the continent, and France is in a strategically ideal position to promote the construction of a distinctively French framework for the new order. The Gaullist ideal of establishing a deterrence/defense structure characterized by both a strong national identity and a strong European identity would appear to be more achievable in 1991 than at any time in the past quarter century. The fundamental debate of the 1960s between cooperation and integration as bases for European security has been re-opened, and odds would seem to favor cooperation, as envisioned by the French. Nevertheless, French reactions to the implications of political change in Europe have been considerably less optimistic.

In an article in the French weekly *L'Express*, Jean-Marc Gonin writes, "On 9 November 1989, the day the Berlin Wall collapsed, a block of concrete fell in France's garden." Adding to what appears to be increasing French pessimism, he observes, "France has lost its leverage." French nuclear deterrent strategy, European leadership, and *droit de regard* over Germany all seemed to lose significance, according to Gonin, over the course of four months.[1] Another writer laments, "France is little by little waking up to the probable consequences of the post-Yalta period. . . . The Gaullist dreams of a Europe run politically by a nuclear France are over."[2] Why the lack of confidence in France's potential leading role in European security?

The answer stems from domestic factors which would likely obstruct firm initiative on the part of France's leaders. As in NATO, so in France, the acceleration of change in the European political scene will reveal ambiguities in security doctrines and the fault lines beneath the apparent consensus supporting those doctrines. Unearthing dissent in political as well as popular circles could have a paralyzing effect on policy-making. Unwillingness to disrupt an increasingly fragile illusion of consensus would reinforce inertia.

What Jane Stromseth has written about flexible response and NATO is equally applicable to Gaullist security doctrine and France: "In seeming to be all things to all people, the compromise of flexible response [Gaullism] allowed NATO [France] to mask—but not resolve—the clash of views in the Alliance [the country]."[3] The ambiguity of Gaullism has invited multiple interpretations, not only of the defense-deterrence balance, but also of the national-supranational and the European-Atlantic balances. Preserving the appearance of consensus has relied heavily on maintaining this ambiguity.

Were French policy-makers to push too forcefully for a more robust conventional defense, they might be accused of betraying the primacy of deterrence. On the other hand, were they to elevate the importance of the *force de frappe* to the apparent neglect of conventional forces, they might be accused of compromising solidarity with France's European allies, thereby betraying de Gaulle's vision of unified Western Europe. Similarly, calling for a unified West European defense might provoke concern in some French circles about loss of autonomy in decision-making, while emphasizing national autonomy too much would prompt fear of isolation from the rest of Europe. As Philippe Le Prestre notes, "If there is agreement on the vague and unassailable principles of independence, fidelity to alliances, and nuclear-based deterrence, there is little agreement over methods to define and operationalize them."[4]

It is difficult to win public support in any country for complex, subtle policies that may appear to conflict with ideology. (Witness, for instance, the failure of *détente* in the United States in the early 1970s.) The tendency, in France as elsewhere, is for policy to be interpreted in political and popular circles in simple, polar, "either-or" terms. For example, national independence and tight integration in defense stand as two identifiable extremes. France's efforts to implement a policy based on greater defense cooperation in Europe might not be appreciated in France as an attempt to achieve a subtle balance between the two extremes, but rather as an overture toward one extreme, the very integration against which General de Gaulle had warned. As Pierre Hassner notes, "If doctrinal rigidity and diplomatic flexibility, apparent simplicity and actual ambiguity constituted a good recipe, it is much more difficult for recognition of complexity and renunciation of ambiguity to coexist."[5]

For a quarter century France was able to avoid steering the narrow course between the multiple imperatives of Gaullist security policy. While France did not really lose the security debate of the 1960s, as noted at the end of chapter one, the influence it retained derived from its status as a counter-model to the leadership the United States was exercising in NATO. In the latter part of de Gaulle's presidency and in the immediate post–de Gaulle period, France had to do very little in order to support its special political leverage as a state within NATO but outside the integrated military command. Rhetoric served its ends as well as any concrete policy. As Robert Grant observes, "The French consider declaratory initiatives to be in and of themselves an important dimension of policy."[6] In the 1960s and 1970s French declarations did pay some short-term political dividends. But in the 1990s and beyond, as France faces an opportunity to turn the rhetoric into long-term reality, it is likely to balk.

In the heyday of American-led security in Europe, France could demand an alternative structure for defense without bearing the responsibility for implementing it. France could maintain its distinctive status in Europe as the loyal opposition while avoiding commitments that might expose divergent domestic views on foreign security policy. In the future, however, given the opportunity to lead, France will have to make the unsavory choice between playing its hand and continuing to hide it. Choosing the former, France would risk widespread dissent at home. Choosing the latter, as is likely, France would pass up the opportunity to shape the security order in a new Europe.

In fact, according to Anton DePorte, twice in the past decade France has neglected opportunities to set Europe on the course of a new security order. He argues that in the early 1980s, as superpower rivalry peaked, and in the mid-to-late 1980s, as a new superpower *détente* evolved, France could have reasserted the Gaullist concept of security. But in neither case "have French leaders seized the evident leadership opportunities offered them to insist that France, and Western Europe, define and defend their own particular interests in the face of the challenges to them."[7]

In the same ironic way that American scholars and statesmen may pine for the "good old days" of the Cold War, when it was clear who the enemy was and the United States stood as ideological leader in the West, so the French may look nostalgically on a time when NATO was strong and when France could reap the political benefits, both at home and in Europe, from demanding an alternative security framework, knowing full well that it would not have to face the consequences of making it reality. As André Brigot writes, "As far as their security interests are concerned, the French do not need change in Europe; or, to be less contentious, they do not perceive the links between these developments and their own collective or individual interests."[8] However, there is a fundamental difference between the American and the French outlooks: The United States looks back on what it perceives as the golden age of American leadership in the West and looks grimly ahead to leadership on the decline, which it will try to forestall. France looks back on an age of strong Gaullist rhetoric, which established the philosophical framework for eventual French leadership in European security, and looks ahead to the opportunity for realization of that leadership, which, by failing to act forcefully and coherently, it will probably lose. Clearly, from a national perspective, the French case is the more tragic. It is better to have led and lost than never to have led at all.

This chapter will discuss the ambiguities surrounding Gaullist security doctrine and, specifically, the place of the *force de frappe* in that doctrine. I will try to describe the different lines of interpretation that have coexisted as long as the French concept has remained at the level of rhetoric. I will then explain how, as France is less able to support ambiguity in its policy, these differences are becoming increasingly manifest in the specific priorities which various leaders in the French government assign top status for the country's future security agenda. Disputes over the defense budget and allocation of declining resources, especially, reflect the type of internal dissent on fundamental questions that may paralyze French initiative in defining a new shape for European security. Finally, I will discuss the much vaunted French consensus on defense and its questionable ability to withstand an unambiguous French commitment to a leading role in Europe.

AMBIGUITIES OF THE
GAULLIST LEGACY

Today in France there is still an imperative across the political spectrum for legislators and government officials to cast policy initiatives in a Gaullist idiom. As the Fifth Republic is just over thirty years old, referring to the precepts of its founding father to justify a course of action naturally enhances legitimacy. However, there are multiple interpretations of Gaullism, and each tendency in the security debate is able to find something in the statements of the General to support its thesis. At the rhetorical level, Gaullism is able to accommodate diverse points of view. The prospect of trying to implement an unambiguous, concrete Gaullist approach to European security, however, must inevitably favor one reading over others and, therefore, reveal the dissenting interpretations, hence, the perceived risk of undermining domestic support for French defense policy.

The last chapter described what seems to be a historically consistent approach to security that the Mitterrand presidency would adopt if it were to take advantage of the emerging opportunity. What will probably preclude such initiative is the fear that individual elements of that approach will not be universally perceived as true to the Gaullist legacy. Generically, the fault lines that might erupt in the French "consensus" are characterized by three schools of interpretation of Gaullism, which can be broadly labeled as nationalist, Europeanist, and pragmatist.

The nationalists cite the primacy de Gaulle attached to the state and define this as the standard by which to measure policy initiatives. They point, for instance to de Gaulle's statement in 1959 that "if one really ceased considering the defense of France in the national context and merged it with something else, it would be impossible for us to maintain a State."[9] From this point of view, any French leadership in European security that would require some integrative institutional form would be untenable, as a formal structure would dilute national identity unacceptably. Parties as politically different as the Communists (PC) and the Gaullist Rassemblement pour la République (RPR) have adopted this line of reasoning.

Speaking before the National Assembly in October 1989, for instance, Communist Deputy Jean-Claude Gayssot observed that until recently "only the Communist deputies had opposed the Franco-German Treaty, *which seriously compromises the independence of our country*" (my emphasis).[10] As described in chapter three, of the various dimensions which would characterize a French-shaped European security order, the Franco-German relationship would allow a high degree of cooperation while preserving the greatest degree of autonomy next to total independence. It is for this reason that France is willing to conduct force planning and joint exercises at that level but not at the NATO level. The Communists' objection to the relationship, coupled with their proclaimed dedication to the "independence and sovereignty" of France's defense, reflects how literally they have adopted the nationalist line of the Gaullist idiom. They link their belief in independence of defense to an agenda favoring French leadership in multi-lateral European disarmament, nuclear as well as conventional. By pronouncing their support for an extremely nationalist interpretation of Gaullism, it seems the Communists would hope to put their patriotism beyond question and thereby garner support for a potentially unpopular initiative of disarmament.

At the other end of the political spectrum, the RPR adopts the same line of reasoning to promote a completely different agenda. Responding to President Mitterrand's decision of May 1989 to cut expenditures on military equipment by approximately 45 billion francs below funds authorized in the 1987–1991 program law, former Prime Minister Jacques Chirac accused the president of "an insidious questioning of our defense. . . . Under the Gaullist varnish of [Mitterrand's] discourse," Chirac wrote in Le Monde, "the insidious questioning of a defense policy which had guaranteed the independence, security and rank of our country, while inspiring the support of the vast majority of French people, is visible."[11] In this illustration, as in the Communist argument, the speaker claims his nationalist line as representing the true legacy of de Gaulle; but the agenda Chirac promotes is diametrically opposed to the Communists'. He cites the theme of national independence in security, not to support the priority of disarmament, but to defend the position that under no conditions can France reduce the financial level of its commitment to defense.

As the European Community approaches its goal of unification by the end of 1992, the RPR has been invoking the nationalist interpretation of Gaullism to counter the tendency toward Euro-federalism. At a national party conference in December 1990, the RPR adopted a "manifesto for the union of European states" that favored a pan-European confederation over any sort of exclusive supranationalism in the West. As RPR President Jacques Chirac stated, "We refuse the concept . . . of a 'federation' of the Twelve, the others being relegated to a vague confederation."[12] By supporting the looser confederation as the primary forum for cooperation for all European states, French conservatives would hope to protect national autonomy of defense against integration. France's independence of decision-making will be more fully preserved by a widening of Europe—"from the Atlantic to the Urals"—loosely structured than by a deepening of the European Community, according to the nationalist interpreters of Gaullism.

The Europeanist interpreters of de Gaulle point to a fundamental flaw in the reasoning of the nationalists, both Left and Right. They observe, as American analyst David Yost has argued, that extreme nationalists have confused as a "policy of independent defense" the Gaullist concept of an "independent defense policy."[13] Unlike an independent defense, the original sense of the concept of an independent policy, according to the Europeanists, does not preclude developing cooperation with allies.[14]

However, as we have already seen, the Europeanists are far from united in their views. While all proponents of Europeanism advocate some form of coordination of defense policies on the continent, the question of degree is critical. There are fundamental differences between the vision of cooperation and the vision of integration in Europe. The concept of West European cooperation in a Gaullist framework, as advocated by the Mitterrand presidency, was described extensively in the last chapter. It is important to recognize that the integrationist line of reasoning also appeals to Gaullism for support. While Jean-Paul Pigasse's prediction, as cited at the beginning of chapter three, of a return to the European Defense Community is described as a liberation from "Gaullist dogma," others justify the integrationist option from within the Gaullist idiom. Dominique Moïsi, editor of the journal *Politique Etrangère*, for example, explains Western Europe's current transition as the realization of "Charles de Gaulle's vision of a world dominated by nations that transcend superficial ideological divisions." Notably, he speaks of de Gaulle and Jean Monnet in the same breath, suggesting that in the late Twentieth Century the federalist concept of Monnet can be seen as compatible with the more loosely cooperative concept of de Gaulle.[15] Although the differences among Europeanists may be less sharply defined than those between nationalists and Europeanists, the divisions within the latter school of thought would come into bolder relief were France to commit to an unambiguous plan in shaping a new European security order.

Finally, there is a line of reasoning which interprets Gaullist philosophy as essentially pragmatic. This reading of de Gaulle's legacy maintains that France is not permanently bound to either independence, cooperation, or integration as a single guiding principle for its security policy. Rather, dogma should take a back seat to *realpolitik*. As Carl Amme wrote in 1967, "De Gaulle is above all a realist. If he sees that his policies may result in isolating France and in decreasing French influence in the affairs of Europe and the world, he could well modify his position."[16] A State Department memorandum to President Kennedy in July 1963, analyzing the probability that de Gaulle would accede to a Partial Test Ban Treaty in exchange for American aid to France's nuclear program, thus characterized de Gaulle's philosophy: "In all his writings, General de Gaulle has consistently condemned leaders who allow themselves to be swayed from their goals by concessions or by such sentiments as gratitude, friendship, etc. Such leaders he regards as traitors to their mission. *But he has also written that a leader must carefully assess the relationship between his means and his ends*" (my emphasis).[17]

Four years later, France would display pragmatic means-ends rationale in negotiating for itself a new relationship vis-à-vis the Atlantic Alliance. In December 1967, while General Charles Ailleret was publicly articulating the *tous azimuts* doctrine for the *force de frappe*, according to which France should be able to target its nuclear weapons against potential threats coming from any geographical direction, including even the West, he was privately making arrangements with SACEUR, General Lyman Lemnitzer, on French cooperation with NATO.[18] A declaratory policy catering to the nationalist line of reasoning combined with a less publicized diplomacy acknowledging necessary coordination of continental security reflected Gaullist understanding, according to the pragmatists' interpretation, that French security could not be founded on one unyielding line of ideology. General François Valentin explains this pragmatism as an appreciation for both long-term and short-term needs. Where different dimensions of the Gaullist legacy appear to be at cross-purposes, they are often responding to particular needs at different times.[19]

A pragmatist's explanation is also offered for the policy of non-automaticity of French commitment to forward defense in Western

Europe. Some have argued that de Gaulle encouraged this dimension of security policy during the Vietnam era out of concern for the seemingly excessive inclination of the United States to intervene militarily in crises. At the time, fear that France might be drawn into a war against its interests as a result of automatic commitment to NATO may have warranted a doctrine of non-automaticity. However, the pragmatic argument continues, the United States has learned its lesson since Vietnam, and in an Alliance where responsibilities are more evenly distributed between Europe and North America, France should be able to integrate more fully without fear of compromising its autonomy.[20]

The French government offered a similar logic to explain its military intervention in the Persian Gulf war of 1991. Many conservatives opposed that intervention for fear that it would reveal a lack of autonomy and essential reliance on the United States. One prominent RPR figure, Alain Juppé, warned in November 1990 that France should protect "its autonomy of decision and not be led into an intervention that it did not choose itself."[21] The President's response to this criticism was that the particular circumstances demanded cooperation, and that while France was contributing to an international military coalition, it was maintaining autonomy of decision-making over French forces, even if those forces came under allied operational control. Had France not intervened in the crisis, declared President Mitterrand, "there would have been a terrible absence in the conscience of the French people, the absence of History."[22] If Gaullism cautions against dependence on other countries it also stresses the importance of national rank and prestige. In the case of the war in the Gulf, the pragmatists' interpretation of Gaullism would permit adaptation of policy according to prevailing circumstances. Appearances of autonomy might be sacrificed in order to establish an important French role at a critical moment in development of the new international order.

Of course, both the nationalists and the Europeanists see their interpretations as pragmatic. They tend, however, to justify their respective agenda in ideological terms and refer to pragmatism only when, on particular issues, their positions might seem to contradict the general trend of their ideological bent. For instance, while Chirac and other Gaullists stand for the strongly nationalist, independent line, many of them also supported the creation of the FAR. That particular position might have seemed to compromise the priority of independence in defense at a moment when many others saw the FAR as a French overture toward closer ties with NATO's military structure. Therefore, in defending his support for the mobile force, Chirac argued, "Gaullism is not a refusal of solidarity. The military doctrine devised in the 1950s and 1960s must be adopted to the evolution of the world, to the evolution of the East-West balance of power, to the evolution of technology, and to the evolution of thinking in Europe."[23]

The pragmatists' interpretation of Gaullism thus adds immensely to the ambiguity of French security doctrine, as it facilitates a crisscrossing of nationalist and Europeanist lines of reasoning. To reiterate, this condition is domestically tenable as long as Gaullism remains at the level of rhetoric; trying actually to implement a Gaullist security policy for Europe, however, will inevitably antagonize one or more of the diverse schools of thought, and this, French leaders fear, might provoke a serious internal crisis.

GAULLISM AND NUCLEAR DETERRENCE

The one issue that most vividly reflects the ambiguities of Gaullism and which is likely to provoke the most disagreement among different points of view in France is the future of the *force de frappe*. Whether or not France does initiate a new course for European security, the prospect of conventional and nuclear disarmament on a grand scale will undoubtedly stir contention within France and between France and the rest of Europe over the continued deployment of French nuclear forces. As the presence of the *force de frappe* becomes ever more conspicuous, external pressures on France to participate in nuclear arms control and internal pressures acting in multiple directions (pressing for arms control, nuclear modernization, *status quo*, etc.) would grow increasingly forceful. As John G. Mason notes, "The international conjuncture that allowed the French exceptional autonomy for their nuclear policies and immunity from international criticism may well be coming to an end."[24]

In an apparent effort to preempt such an eventuality, the French have argued that in the new Europe, at lower conventional force levels, pure deterrence (i.e., massive retaliation) will take on a new and greater importance. Furthermore, they maintain, the role of the *force de frappe* as a European deterrent will acquire increased relevance as the United States withdraws from Europe, and especially if there is a mutual reduction or elimination of NATO and Warsaw Pact short-range nuclear forces. Domestic French agreement on these principles, however, is not matched by agreement on how to put them into practice. If France is to convince the rest of Europe of the continued need for a nationally controlled French nuclear force, it must first be able to establish a firm, popularly supported stance at home, and that is unlikely to happen.

The potential for dissent in France over the capabilities needed to support its nuclear doctrine became vividly apparent at the time of the superpower agreement on elimination of intermediate-range nuclear forces (INF). In a display of European solidarity, President Mitterrand had expressed his support in early 1988 for the achievement of the 1987 Washington Treaty. He cast his position in typically Gaullist language, explaining to American Senator Robert Byrd, for instance, that he opposed intermediate-range missiles in general, as they create the perception of weaker resolve to use the strategic deterrent.[25] Furthermore, in subsequent interviews Mitterrand expressed reservations about the modernization of American short-range nuclear missiles (less than 500 km range) remaining in Europe, possibly implying support for a "third zero."[26] Some analysts inferred from this position that following his reelection in the spring of that year, Mitterrand might call for cancellation of France's own *Hadès* prestrategic nuclear missile, scheduled to replace the *Pluton* in 1992.[27] Such an initiative would have seemed consistent with the trend of France's drawing closer to its neighbors' security policies. However, the Europeanist intent eventually backfired.

Ironically, as French analyst Pierre Hassner observed, while political divisions in other European countries were disappearing, Mitterrand's support for the INF Treaty and the implication that he might favor a third zero served to highlight a rift between Right and Left in France.[28] Having at first kept silent on his disagreement with the INF Treaty, conservative Prime Minister Jacques Chirac drew the line when Mitterrand seemed to take a stand against short-range nuclear force modernization, as this could have a direct bearing on the future of France's own force. In a press conference in early March 1988, Chirac announced his strong opposition to a third zero. He articulated a nationalist explanation for his stance, arguing that the modernization of NATO's short-range nuclear forces should not concern France, given French status outside the integrated military structure. He added that France fully intended to modernize its own prestrategic nuclear force by continuing to fund the *Hadès* program.[29] Also, former Defense Minister André Giraud responded to

Mitterrand's statements by calling on France to compensate for the INF Treaty by filling the vacuum in Europe with French intermediate-range forces.[30]

The potential for a serious crisis in the government over this issue led Mitterrand to shift from a Europeanist to a pragmatic line of reasoning. Following on the heels of Chirac's press conference, Mitterrand's advisors "clarified" that the president had not implied that there should be a third zero but rather that modernization was not urgent at that time.[31] To prevent a potential rupture in France's cohabitation leadership, Mitterrand compromised on his Europeanist stance. Ultimately, not only did this dispute reveal internal political differences on the issue of short-range nuclear modernization, it also worked against Mitterrand's efforts at European solidarity. The president's "clarification" of his statements alluding to a third zero, combined with his explanation that his support for the INF Treaty had been based on an interest in enhancing the credibility of strategic deterrence, led France to look inward toward its own nuclear capability instead of outward toward Europe.[32]

Moreover, tension in France over the need for short-range nuclear weapons did not go away immediately. Even after Mitterrand's reelection in the spring of 1988, the fate of the *Hadès* missile had not been definitively resolved. A visit by Michel Rocard to an army exercise at Canjuers in the South of France, his first as prime minister, in early March 1989, reminded the French public that questions remained about the role of prestrategic nuclear weapons. Notably, Rocard had requested that the exercise not include the Leclerc tank or the *Hadès* missile. Ostensibly the reason for this request was that these systems were not yet deployed with the First Army. However, neither were certain other systems included in the demonstration, such as the multiple launch rocket system (MLRS) and Super-Puma helicopter. In fact, even the *Pluton* missile, which is currently deployed with the army, was not included. Despite Rocard's explanations, it was clear that he was making a political statement. Later the prime minister alluded to the *Hadès* as "falling in the realm of systems conceptually difficult to treat as prestrategic."[33] Rocard seemed to be taking the position that Mitterrand had taken a year before.

Domestically, the issue was resolved (at least temporarily) at the president's press conference of 20 May 1989. Mitterrand confirmed plans to build the *Hadès* and reaffirmed that it "could be used only for

the final warning shot, and not as a battlefield or theater weapon."[34]
Crisis at home was, for the moment, forestalled. Whether this condition
will hold permanently is questionable. Since May 1989 the conservative
opposition has begun to challenge the Mitterrand administration's silence on a program to modernize France's land-based strategic deterrent.[35]

The insistence from some political circles on the need for a new
missile to replace the eighteen aging S3 intermediate-range ballistic
missiles on the *plateau d'Albion* reveals yet another difference in
perception of the operational needs of pure deterrence. On this issue,
as on *Hadès*, the potential for a tear in the delicate fabric of the so-called
consensus is becoming visible.

The issue of replacing the land-based leg of France's strategic
deterrent has prompted proposals from different camps. Supporters of
former Defense Minister Chevènement favor abandoning the *plateau
d'Albion* and funding a long-range air-launched cruise missile, possibly
in cooperation with the British. Conservatives, wary of putting all of
France's nuclear eggs in one basket (or two, including the sea-based
deterrent) call for funding of an air-based missile as well as a mobile,
land-based S45 missile. This plan, they argue, will hedge against future
increased vulnerability and will also be more tenable politically. A
third option, described in the last chapter, was put before the National
Assembly in June 1991 by an advisor to Defense Minister Pierre Joxe.
Similar to the conservatives' proposal, it calls for an air-land-sea triad.
However, the new land-based leg would consist not of a mobile S45,
but rather of a fixed, multi-warhead missile, modeled after the new M-5
sea-based missile.[36]

Chevènement praises the air-based option (*air-sol loine portée*—
ASLP) for its flexibility. It combines the best of both worlds, according
to its supporters, preserving French national control while emphasizing
European-wide protection through the option of shifting bombers' bases
within Europe and through cooperative production with the British.[37]
S45 supporters, such as former Defense Minister André Giraud, argue
that ease of relocation is precisely why the ASLP would not make a
good deterrent. A land-based deterrent fixed in France, however, has
the advantage of "obliging the enemy to take responsibility for a first
direct strike." The greater risk thereby implied makes a land-based
deterrent more credible, according to this argument, which also cites
greater vulnerability, slowness of response, and technical problems,

such as in-flight refueling, as reasons to doubt the effectiveness of the ASLP.[38] The issue has been hotly debated under the pressures of time and shrinking budgets, and both sides adduce nationalist and Europeanist cases for their respective causes.

Interestingly, supporters of a new land-based missile claim an important goal of the project is to achieve improved accuracy in the new generation of the deterrent. Yet, French nuclear doctrine ostensibly calls for simple, anti-city, massive retaliation. The *force de frappe* should, therefore, require minimal modernization, other than regular maintenance and possible improvement in penetration capability and survivability. Why, then, would an anti-city deterrent require enhanced accuracy? Why does France need, as Jacques Chirac argues, "a land-based mobile missile, capable of reaching military targets in the Soviet Union?"[39]

The rationale behind the conservative argument may rest, once again, on adoption of the pragmatic interpretation of Gaullism. As analyst Jane Stromseth observes, "Given French resources and technology in the 1960s, a counter-city strategy was the only feasible option for the French nuclear force."[40] Such a strategy, conservatives could argue, was not intended to be etched in stone, but was only a pragmatic recognition of capabilities available at the time. In fact, Chirac, RPR Deputy François Fillon, and others would assert, Gaullism demands that nuclear doctrine advance with technology; by postponing a decision on the future of the land-based deterrent, therefore, the Socialists would be betraying the Gaullist legacy.

Dissent on this very basic point—the essential capabilities, both strategic and prestrategic, required to fulfill the Gaullist concept of deterrence—would become even more heated if France were to try to implement a Europeanization of the *force de frappe* by, for instance, sharing targeting information with allies and/or introducing measures for multi-national consultation before a national decision to launch nuclear weapons would be made in crisis or war. Steps France would have to take in order to reassure its neighbors would rekindle thinly veiled domestic differences.

Like the United States, France faces the challenge of convincing its allies that a nationally controlled nuclear force can provide extended deterrence. It bears the double burden of guaranteeing the other European states that the *force de frappe* would definitely be launched in a crisis or war when it would be in their common interests, and that under no circumstances would nuclear weapons otherwise be launched. What is more, in the current political environment this dilemma is compounded by an imperative to justify the need for deterrence at all, particularly deterrence based on missiles that would land in the now friendly, democratizing countries of Central Europe.

Ultimately, one country's belief that another country's nationally operated nuclear deterrent would be used absolutely in the first country's vital interests must rest on trust. As General Georges Fricaud-Chagnaud, Director of the Fondation pour les études de défense nationale, argues, there is no declaration of policy that can substitute for this trust. The difference between American and French extended deterrence is less a function of stated policy than of the simple fact that "nothing will make the Rhine as wide as the Atlantic." The idea that the *force de frappe*, unlike the American strategic nuclear force, can be considered a European deterrent rests fundamentally on the "geographic and political continuity of Europe."[41] If France's neighbors accepted this existential argument at face value, then France might be able to achieve its goal of making the *force de frappe* the centerpiece of European security without disrupting internal "consensus." However, from its allies' point of view, French statements and policy initiatives may be able to increase or decrease the relative trust.

For instance, in the early 1980s, the definition of French security interests by then Defense Minister Charles Hernu raised doubts in Europe about French commitment to extended deterrence. Hernu framed French interests in terms of "three circles" (not to be confused with the circles of security relationships described in the last chapter): the national sanctuary, Europe, and the rest of the world. Anything outside of French national territory Hernu described as "contingent interests."[42] This formulation, emphasizing the distinction between France and the rest of Europe, prompted concern as to when the French would use their nuclear weapons. In a crisis, would they actually wait until Germany had been overrun to fire the final warning shot? While the idea of trading Paris for Berlin may inherently have marginally greater credibility than the idea of trading Washington for Berlin, Hernu's statement did not enhance that credibility.

One might expect that actions would speak louder than words in convincing Europe of French commitment to extended deterrence. However, as discussed above, when French leaders enter the realm of actions they risk domestic crisis stemming from internal confrontation over the dos and don'ts of Gaullist security policy. In the early 1980s the Mitterrand administration had considered deploying prestrategic nuclear weapons on German soil under a dual-key arrangement. Eventually Paris backed down, constrained by the limits of permissible initiative. Today, particularly as Europe questions the need for nuclear weapons at all in a "common European house," it would seem, as Pierre Hassner argues, that "France will only make its allies, notably Germany, see the European role of its deterrent force if it is willing to engage with them at the conventional level, both in the forward battle [or some alternative operational posture, as the case may be in a unified Germany] and in arms control negotiations."[43] The degree of integration that would be required, however, would be unacceptable from a domestic point of view. Even if the French were able to agree on an unambiguous doctrine and operational concept for the *force de frappe*, a shaky proposition to begin with, the compromises they would have to make in order to allay other countries' fears would expose more domestic fissures.

Until now, France has been able to stave off a crisis over the *force de frappe*. Occasional near-crises have brought the potential fault lines to the surface, but they have not erupted. Through ambiguous Gaullist rhetoric, the Mitterrand leadership has been able to preserve the balance between internal and external pressures on the nuclear deterrent. Whether rhetoric alone will be able to serve this purpose in the future is doubtful. If the *force de frappe* is to become a European deterrent, France's neighbors will probably insist that France support its declaratory policy with actions, such as tighter integration in European security and perhaps (what would be the most untenable proposition to the French) multi-lateral control. Alternatively, if the nuclear force remains a deterrent over the national sanctuary only, France is likely to isolate itself inadvertently from European security. A firm European nuclear policy would not be able to sustain an illusory consensus. Finally, even if ambiguous statements on how the *force de frappe* would become Europeanized can temporarily reconcile internal differences on that aspect of French security policy, dissent is less easily quieted on other related issues, most notably the defense budget.

DEBATE ON THE DEFENSE BUDGET

Since 1989, debate on the military program law has become an important channel for differences over the operationalization of French

security doctrine. Differences that could be hidden by ambiguous
rhetoric when announcing doctrine could not be suppressed when
allocating limited resources to defense. Currently, it is in the budgeting
process that fissures in the consensus seem to be most loudly vocalized.
The open dissent on that issue may be a foretaste of what the government
should expect if it tries to forge a strong leading French role in shaping
the future of European security.

According to one report, from 1981 to 1985 annual economic growth
in France averaged 1.1 percent, one of the lowest rates of growth in
Europe.[44] Despite a sluggish economy, in 1987 France adopted what
both Right and Left have since admitted was an ambitious military
program law for the five-year period from 1987 to 1991. Authorized
allocations for military hardware (Title V in the defense budget) over
the five-year period totaled approximately 474 billion francs.[45] The
plan reflected what historian Samy Cohen calls a "principal leitmotif"
of Gaullism: "Yes to reinforcement of the nuclear arm, no to weakening
of the conventional arm."[46] One of its fundamental goals was to raise
defense spending to 4 percent of gross domestic product by 1991.

This goal soon proved unrealistic. In 1988, defense spending accounted for 3.669 percent of GDP and fell to 3.62 percent in 1989.[47]
Following the election of a Socialist majority to the National Assembly
in the spring of 1988, ending the two-year period of Socialist-RPR cohabitation, the new government proposed a revision of the military program law. How much to reduce defense spending was an intra-Socialist
dispute for the first part of 1989, pitting Defense Minister Chevènement
against Prime Minister Rocard and Finance Minister Pierre Bérégovoy.
President Mitterrand eventually made the final decision in a May press
conference, announcing that Title V spending should be reduced by 40
to 45 billion francs for the period from 1990 to 1993, but that cuts
should not touch "major arms programs," the loss of which would
jeopardize France's "rank."[48] While this constituted a smaller savings
than Rocard and Bérégovoy had hoped for (they had encouraged reduction to below 400 billion francs) it was enough to provoke the
conservative opposition. When the revised program law for 1990 to
1993 came before the National Assembly in October 1989, debate was
fierce.

Deputies' arguments pointed less to particular strategic deficiencies
than to the impact of proposed cuts on the fundamental integrity of
France's basic (Gaullist) security doctrine. Debate focused not on
military issues but rather on which law was more faithful to the

primacy of deterrence and which would be more likely to preserve popular consensus. Speaking before the National Assembly, for instance, RPR Deputy André Berthol observed that, although ambitious, the 1987–1991 program law had been realistic, while the new proposal would deal a serious blow to national consensus, independence of defense, and army morale.[49] One of the most vocal critics was RPR Deputy François Fillon, former chairman of the Defense Commission of the National Assembly. Fillon condemned as "impossible" Mitterrand's goal of cutting 45 billion francs from defense spending without touching major programs, noting in particular that probable cuts would result in a qualitative decline in the future capabilities of the army. "By choosing not to choose," he argued, "the President of the Republic risks not being able to sustain France's rank."[50] "Rank" and similar key political themes were the criteria against which detractors measured the new program law. Furthermore, they tended to cite the unanimous vote by which the 1987–1991 program law had passed, along with Mitterrand's endorsement of that law as "realistic, coherent, and reasonable," and asked why the Socialists had decided now to back down from that mandate.[51]

In fact, Socialist support for an ambitious, conservative program law during the period of cohabitation may have represented a last attempt to prolong the appearance of consensus before yielding to the constraints of limited resources. Jean-Michel Boucheron explains that "the two years '87–'88 separating the legislative and presidential elections were perceived as a parenthesis by the majority at the time, a period during which it could undertake projects that, regardless of the results of the presidential elections, would be reexamined shortly anyway."[52] The peculiar condition of cohabitation tended to heighten caution within the government and legislature for fear that a rupture over national security issues might turn into a devastating crisis for the Fifth Republic.

The Constitution of 1958 and subsequent ordinances of 1959 and 1971 do not clearly distinguish between the authority of the president and the authority of the prime minister on issues of national defense.[53] Although popular perception is that the president has the last word on defense (and in practice this is indeed the case) formally there is an ambiguous overlap between his and the prime minister's powers. When the two offices were held by members of the same party, the ambiguous delineation of powers was a non-issue. However, under a Socialist president and a Gaullist prime minister, it was feared that a dispute over decision-making authority in national defense could spark a more widespread national crisis.[54] Therefore, as discussed above in the example of short-range nuclear weapons modernization, leaders bent over backwards to uphold the illusion of consensus.

Asked why in 1987 the Socialists had voted for the 1987–1991 program law, Prime Minister Rocard responded that "a negative vote by the Socialist Party would have been interpreted by the opposition, at the time, as disagreement on the French doctrine of deterrence."[55] Similarly, Socialist Deputy Jean Gatel observed that the unanimity in 1987 referred to broad goals and not to specific policies.[56] Cohabitation had yielded a high degree of inertia in French foreign and security policy. Politics during this period were characterized by "a certain tendency to preempt the foreign policy debate and present the other party with a *fait accompli*."[57] Ironically, during the very years when domestic dissent was most feared, it was avoided, albeit to the detriment of French initiative in European security.

When the crisis appeared to have passed, however, and a Socialist majority was returned to the National Assembly, the need to take special care to protect the consensus was understood to be less imperative, and the political differences that had been restrained for two years broke loose. Today, therefore, the debate that was preempted under cohabitation has returned with a vengeance. Magnified by greater recognition of limited resources, the political dispute over priorities in military procurement has become the current focus of dissent and certainly has the potential of exploding if the French government tries to initiate a concrete plan for a new security order in Europe.

Freed from the constraints of cohabitation, the Socialists have been as damning in their condemnation of the 1987–1991 program law as the RPR and other moderate-to-conservative parties have been in theirs of the 1990–1993 program law.[58] Speaking for the Finance Committee of the National Assembly, Socialist François Hollande criticized the 1987–1991 law as incoherent, designating a lot of programs as "priorities" but making no choices.[59] In an interview in June 1989, then Defense Minister Chevènement observed, "The tragedy is that we want to do with 3.6 percent of our GNP what the Americans do with more than twice that percentage of theirs."[60] The inability to continue saying both "yes to reinforcement of the nuclear arm and no to weakening of the conventional arm" is becoming increasingly evident, and the need to make choices is further exposing an already thinly veiled dissent in French political circles.

The substantive results of the approximately 45-billion-franc cut in Title V defense spending for 1990–1993 will be mostly delays by several months to two years of completion of programs carried over from the 1987–1991 program law and reduced orders for some hardware. A partial list of programs subject to modification includes:[61]

Charles de Gaulle aircraft carrier	2-year delay
Light frigates	1-year delay
Atlantique-2 maritime surveillance aircraft	3 instead of 5 aircraft
3 new attack submarines (SSNs)	18-month delay
New generation nuclear submarine (SSBN)	6-month delay
Rafale fighter (naval version)	2-year delay
New version AMX 30 tank	canceled
New version 155-mm artillery pieces	canceled
Leclerc tank	1,050 instead of 1,400
Orchidée battlefield observation system	1-year delay
Mirage 2000	28 instead of 33 per year
Nuclear tests in Pacific	reduced number
Santal (army logistical transport program)	reduced number

None of these decisions would seem to pull the rug from under French defense doctrine, yet, as mentioned above, this is precisely the accusation the conservative opposition has made. One review of the new program law described the net impact of the alterations as "burying France's strategy of thirty years without replacing it with a new one."[62] A common charge in the National Assembly debate was that the Socialists were undercutting deterrence and France's ability to fulfill its commitment to Europe.[63] If a few delays in deployment schedules have sparked this type of debate, one can imagine the probable reaction to a whole new French initiative in European security.

Following the war in the Persian Gulf, President Mitterrand stressed the importance of France's continuing to modernize its military capability. Meanwhile, senators and deputies dispute a defense budget that hovers just below 3.4 percent of GDP. No one wants to take responsibility for abandoning major systems, and few are willing to admit one of the most important lessons of the Gulf crisis, that national

defense autonomy is becoming less critical than efficient inter-operability among different nations' forces and command structures.

On the other hand, the Gulf war may also have given a new lease on
life to supporters of high defense budgets. To those who saw the end of
the Cold War as a time for reaping peace dividends, conservatives may
now point to the Persian Gulf as an illustration of the type of instability
that will require France to keep up its guard. If the French believe that
their influence in Europe is waning anyway, they may try to cut their
losses by devoting more defense resources to Third World areas in which
they have continued vested interests, particularly the African countries
formerly under French colonial rule.

Unique in Europe, France maintains extensive security arrangements
with countries in the Third World. French territories outside the metro-
polis cover 600,000 square kilometers, inhabited by 1.5 million French
citizens.[64] France has defense agreements with eight African states and
agreements of cooperation with twenty others. In the 1980s it executed
several major intervention operations in Central Africa, Chad, and Togo,
in addition to the assistance it provided to Lebanon, independently and
as part of the United Nations Forces in Lebanon (UNIFIL).[65]

Deputy Jean-Michel Boucheron, in his report on the 1990–1993 program law, pointed out the increasing relevance to international security
of extra-European conflicts. By fulfilling its commitments in the Third
World, he observed, France "is preserving the interests, the security
and the projection of Europe in external theaters."[66] This formulation
establishes an interesting link between French perceptions of France's
roles in security both inside and outside Europe. The idea that French
engagement in the Third World represents European as well as national
interests may suggest an alternative channel for French leadership in
European security. If proposing a blueprint for restructuring security on
the continent implies too great a domestic risk for France, it may see its
contribution to peacekeeping in Africa and the Middle East as an indirect
way to satisfy its aspirations for leadership in Europe. In the first month
of the Gulf crisis (August 1990), the chairman of the Senate Committee
on Foreign Policy, Defense, and Armed Forces argued similarly that in
its intervention France must act as "a country at the forefront of the
security of the European Community."[67]

Greater spending on non-European security interests could cause
France to withdraw further from its leadership opportunity in European
security. Relatively stronger initiative in the Third World would divert

French attention somewhat from Europe and might, therefore, partially substitute for the French government's inability to reconcile domestic political dissent with its ambition for leadership in continental security.

THE FUTURE OF POPULAR CONSENSUS

Ironically, the very popular consensus that French leaders invoke in support of divergent priorities for France's security agenda is as illusory as the consensus within the political class. However, unlike active dissent within the government and legislature, the public displays relative indifference on questions of national defense. The much vaunted national consensus exists less in strong, tangible public support for French defense policy than in the absence of a strong, tangible opposition. The evidence most often cited as proof of consensus, observes Pierre Hassner, is "the weakness of pacifist and, more generally, antinuclear movements" in France.[68] Active support, however, is considerably less impressive than one might infer from National Assembly debates and statements in the press by national leaders.

Indeed, the image of consensus which leaders applaud and insist on protecting through their particular policy agenda may be precisely what sustains indifference. If the French public is led to believe that national consensus is so overwhelming, then why, people may ask, even bother to discuss it, let alone question it? As Socialist Deputy Huguette Bouchardeau observed in addressing the National Assembly during the debate over the 1990–1993 program law, "The consensus . . . has become a sort of postulate which deprives [French] society of all democratic debate. . . . Citizens, if they do not approve the policy of over-arming, are suspected either of being bad Frenchmen, or of being naïve."[69] This "postulate" is self-perpetuating. The more it becomes ingrained in the national psyche, the more it is simply accepted.

In some cases actual apathy on national security issues can be roughly measured. A poll taken in four Western European countries in 1981 and 1982, asking people about their confidence in NATO's ability to deter an attack and its ability to defend against attack, found a considerably higher percentage of "don't know" responses in France than in Great Britain, the FRG, or Italy. The results were as follows:

Percentage Responding "Don't Know"*

	France		Next Highest (FRG)	
	'81	'82	'81	'82
NATO's ability to deter	33	36	15	12
NATO's ability to defend	25	37	14	14

*Stephen F. Szabo, *West European Public Perceptions of Security Issues: A Survey of Attitudes in France, the FRG, Great Britain, and Italy over Three Decades*, Research Report (Washington, DC: U.S. Information Agency, Office of Research, 1988), Appendix B.3 pp. 70-71.

The comparatively high percentage of French respondents who simply had no opinion on this issue, as on others, illustrates the indifference on which the so-called popular consensus is founded.

The weakness of the bond between citizen and national security is further reflected in statistics on national military service. The figure commonly quoted for the number of troops in the French First Army and FAR is around 300,000.[70] However, when one subtracts clerical, administrative and other non-combat personnel, the number of men in arms is closer to 200,000. Moreover, the illusion that national military service is a common denominator, reinforcing the filial bond between the population and the defense of *la patrie*, is at least partially dispelled when one considers that four out of five students with university diplomas manage to get out of serving under arms, (serving, instead, at clerk-type positions). The majority of students in the top schools choose to do a form of cooperation abroad in lieu of military service.[71]

A national poll on defense issues taken in early 1989 further reflected the actual ambivalence in the French consensus. Fifty-seven per cent of respondents indicated support for the *force de frappe*, an increase of 7 percent since 1980. However, only 8 per cent said they would favor launching nuclear weapons if Soviet forces were to invade French territory. What may be even more surprising is that 56 per cent of respondents favored no use of force at all if Soviet forces invaded France, preferring negotiation instead, even at that stage of an attack on the West. (Sixty-seven per cent favored either continued attempt at negotiation or neutrality rather than intervention following a Soviet attack on Germany.)[72] Although these questions and responses may seem absurd in the context of the emerging political climate between East and West, they still serve as good indicators of the lack of a consistent, identifiable spirit of defense in the French population.

The relative indifference of the French population on national security issues, however, does not imply that public opinion can be disregarded in forging a French role in European security. On the contrary, public apathy may be as dependent on the ambiguity of French defense doctrine as is coexistence of divergent interpretations of Gaullism within the political class. A clear shift in France's policy away from rhetoric and toward stronger leadership in European security would surely prompt a public reaction. Thus Pierre Hassner writes, "The political class will only be able to save the essence of consensus through a process of reciprocal adaptation to external constraints and trends in [public] opinion."[73]

Precisely out of concern for public reaction, past French overtures toward greater cooperation with NATO were executed with utmost secrecy. For example, all copies of documents relating to contingency plans for French support of United States forces returning to Europe were numbered, and officers at Supreme Headquarters Allied Powers Europe and in the office of the chief of staff of the French armed forces knew who had each one. This was done to preserve the image of independence of defense decision-making for the French public.[74] Similarly, French officials insisted on maintaining secrecy in an offer to make ammunition storage igloos in France, formerly used by Germany, available to the United States. When it was learned that insurance for the materiel to be stockpiled in those igloos would have to be cleared through the United States Congress, the offer was withdrawn, again to avoid a spark that might disrupt popular perception of French security. For the same reason, arrangements made pursuant to a French request for closer coordination of France's Tactical Air Force with NATO air forces were carried out with extreme discretion.

The ends to which the French have gone to preserve what they perceive to be a popular consensus on national defense show that public opinion does indeed matter. Although currently based more on indifference than on active support for French policy, the consensus may be fragile and easily upset by any sudden policy shift by the French leadership, such as a decision to initiate the type of European order described in this analysis. As Hassner remarks, "To engage France . . . in favor of a European strategy that combines the national and the collective, the nuclear and the conventional, defense and *détente*, does not seem to be the kind of program that would have a good chance of mobilizing the masses."[75]

Not only would such a strategy be difficult for the public to understand

and absorb, but it might be misinterpreted as a shift toward integration, in which case an indifferent public, prodded by a conservative political opposition to the President's initiative, could suddenly be motivated to form an active consensus against the trend of security policy. In general, it is concern for just such an eventuality that is likely to prevent France's political leaders from moving beyond Gaullist security rhetoric.

The evolution of the legacy of General de Gaulle has had an ironic effect. Rather than facilitate a leading role for France in the new Europe, it has prompted ambiguities and multiple interpretations which are more likely to keep French heads of state preoccupied trying to balance domestic and foreign pressures on France's security policy. France is thus unlikely to capitalize on its emerging opportunity to lead the construction of a new, cooperative framework for European security.

NOTES

1. Jean-Marc Gonin, "Paris-Bonn: fin de bail," *L'Express* (16 March 1990), p. 46.

2. Olivier Weber in *Le Point*, cited in Edward Cody, "Angst over Germany Spreads to France," *The Washington Post*, 17 March 1990 p. A22.

3. Jane E. Stromseth, *The Origins of Flexible Response* (London, The MacMillan Press, 1988), p. 194.

4. Philippe G. Le Prestre, "The Lessons of Cohabitation," in Philippe G. Le Prestre, ed., *French Security Policy in a Disarming World* (Boulder, CO, Lynne Rienner Publishers, 1989), p. 40.

5. Pierre Hassner, "Un chef-d'oeuvre en péril: le consensus français sur la défense," *Esprit* (March–April 1988), p. 81.

6. Robert Grant, "French Security Policy and the Franco-German Relationship," in Robbin F. Laird, ed., *Strangers and Friends: The Franco-German Security Relationship* (London, Pinter Publishers, 1989), p. 30.

7. Anton W. DePorte, "French Security Policy in Its Domestic and International Settings," in Le Prestre, ed., p. 2.

8. André Brigot, "A Neighbor's Fears: Enduring Issues in Franco-German Relations," in Le Prestre, ed., p. 99.

Also lamenting the irony of France's position, Anne Marie Le Gloannec, a French scholar specializing in French-German relations, observes, "The French leadership thinks we have nothing to gain from overcoming the division of Europe because we'll become a small marginal power living side by side with a mighty German central power." Cited in Alan Riding, "Fear in Paris: Ties to Bonn Will Be Hurt," *The New York Times*, 9 November 1989, p. A13.

9. Cited in Yves Boyer, "The U.S. Military Presence in Europe and French Security Policy," *The Washington Quarterly* (Spring, 1988), p. 204.

10. Jean-Claude Gayssot in Assemblée Nationale de la République Française, "Équipement militaire pour les années 1990–1993," Débats Parlementaires, *Journal officiel de la république française*, 9e Leg., le sess., 2e séance, 3 October 1989, p. 3058.

11. Jacques Chirac, "Une remise en cause insidieuse de notre défense," *Le Monde*, 10 June 1989, p. 1.

12. "Le RPR veut une seule Europe élargie aux pays de l'Est," *Le Monde*, 7 December 1990, p. 9. See also Stanley Hoffmann, "La France dans le nouvel ordre européen," *Politique Etrangère* (no. 3, 1990), p. 507.

13. David S. Yost, *France's Deterrent Posture and Security in Europe—Part I: Capabilities and Doctrine*, Adelphi Paper, 194 (London, International Institute for Strategic Studies, 1984/85), p. 9.

14. The idea of "*gaullisme européen*" found expression in the immediate post–de Gaulle era through the Centre d'analyse et de prévision (CAP), developed by President Georges Pompidou's foreign minister, Michel Jobert. The CAP was created to breathe new life into French foreign policy analysis and supported closer French ties to Europe and the United States, while keeping policy in a Gaullist framework. See Samy Cohen, *La Monarchie nucléaire* (Paris, Hachette, 1986), p. 95.

15. Dominique Moïsi, "Germany's Unity, Europe's Rebirth," *The New York Times*, 20 November 1989, p. A23.

16. Carl H. Amme, *NATO without France: A Strategic Appraisal* (Stanford, Stanford University Press, 1967), p. 35.

17. Robert G. Neumann, *Political Consequences of Possible U.S. Aid to the French Nuclear Program in Exchange for France's Adherence to an Eventual Test Ban Treaty*, Memorandum to Mr. Schlesinger for the President (21 July 1963). NB: All historical documents used in this study are available at the National Security Archive, 1755 Massachusetts Ave., NW, Suite 500, Washington, DC 20036. This will be indicated henceforth as "NSA."

18. François Valentin, "Co-operation between Conventional Forces in Europe: A French View," in Yves Boyer, Pierre Lellouche, and John Roper, eds., *Franco-British Defence Cooperation* (London, Royal Institute of International Affairs, 1988), p. 59.

19. François Valentin, "Quelle défense pour quelle Europe?" *Politique Etrangère* (no. 3, 1990), p. 534.

20. Robert Grant, "French Defense Policy and European Security," in Robbin F. Laird, ed., *French Security Policy from Independence to Interdependence* (Boulder, CO, Westview Press, 1986), p. 18.

21. "M. Juppé (RPR): 'La France doit rester à l'écart de toute action militaire'," *Le Monde*, 8 November 1990, p. 40. See also "M. Chirac regrette

d'avoir approuvé l'opération 'Daguet'," *Le Monde*, 4 October 1990, p. 9.

22. Anne Chaussebourg and Alain Rollat, "M. François Mitterrand réplique à ses censeurs," *Le Monde*, 8 February 1991, p. 8. See also "Le général Schmitt affirme qu'il ne faut pas confondre 'autonomie des forces' et 'autonomie de décision'," *Le Monde*, 21 November 1990, p. 4.

23. Cited in David S. Yost, *France and Conventional Defense in Central Europe* (Boulder, CO, Westview Press, 1985), p. 100.

24. John G. Mason, "Mitterrand, the Socialists, and French Nuclear Policy," in Le Prestre, ed., p. 73.

25. Cited in U.S. Congress, Senate, *The INF Treaty and the Future of the Alliance*, Robert Byrd, Report on a Senate delegation visit to five NATO countries (6–14 February 1988), Delegation headed by Senator Robert Byrd, 100th Cong., 2d Sess., p. 10.

26. Michel Colomès and Philippe Chatenay, "Défense: ententes forcées," *Le Point* (7 March 1988), p. 38.

27. Robert Rudney, "Mitterrand Reelection Threatens Mobile S-4, *Hadès* Missiles," *Armed Forces Journal International* (July 1988), p. 32.

28. Hassner, p. 72.

29. Colomès and Chatenay, p. 39.

30. Cited in Jolyon Howorth, "French Defence: Disarmament and Deterrence," *The World Today* (June 1988), p. 105.

31. Colomès and Chatenay, p. 39.

32. Hassner, p. 72.

33. Jacques Isnard, "Une armée de terre sans ses missiles nucléaires," *Le Monde*, 4 March 1989, p. 13.

34. "Le conférence de presse du Président de la République," *Le Monde*, 20 May 1989, p. 7.

35. Assemblée Nationale de la République Française, *Avis présenté au nom de la commission des affaires étrangères sur le projet de loi de finances pour 1990 (no. 895)*, Tome XI, Défense. No. 922, Opinion prepared by Claude-Gérard Marcus, 9e Leg., le sess., 12 October 1989, p. 11. See also Chirac, p. 1.

36. Cited in Jacques Isnard, "Un conseiller de M. Joxe plaide pour le maintien de la 'triade' nucléaire," *Le Monde*, 19 June 1991, p. 12. The advisor also proposed that the *plateau d'Albion* be put under army control, because the air force would now be responsible for the long-range air-launched leg of the deterrent.

37. Jacques Isnard, "M. Mitterrand devrait choisir entre un missile mobile et un système d'arme nucléaire adapté à l'avion Rafale," *Le Monde*, 16 January 1991, p. 16.

38. André Giraud, "Nos armes nucléaires," *Le Monde*, 16 January 1991, p. 2.

39. Chirac, p. 1.

40. Stromseth, p. 100.

41. Georges Fricaud-Chagnaud, "French Nuclear Deterrence and European Solidarity," in Laird, ed., *French Security Policy*, p. 125.

42. Charles Hernu, "La sécurité de la France: équilibre, dissuasion, volonté," Discours à l'IHEDN, 15 November 1983, in Charles Hernu, *Défendre la paix* (Paris, J. C. Lattès, 1985), pp. 27–28.

43. Hassner, p. 80.

44. Organization for Economic Cooperation and Development (OECD) report, cited in Edward A. Kolodziej, "British-French Nuclearization and European Denuclearization: Implications for U.S. Policy," in Le Prestre, ed., p. 130.

45. Assemblée Nationale de la République Française, *Rapport fait au nom de la commission de la défense nationale et des forces armées sur le projet de loi de programmation (no. 432) relatif à l'équipement militaire pour les années 1987–1991*, No. 622, Report prepared by François Fillon, 8e Leg., 2e sess., 7 April 1987, p. 69.

46. Cohen, p. 208.

47. Assemblée Nationale de la République Française, *Rapport fait au nom de la commission de la défense nationale et des forces armées sur le projet de loi de programmation (no. 733) relatif à l'équipement militaire pour les années 1990–1993*, No. 897, Report prepared by Jean-Michel Boucheron, 9e Leg., le sess., 2 October 1989, p. 162 (hereafter cited as Boucheron, *Rapport*).

48. "Le conférence de presse du Président de la République," *Le Monde*, 20 May 1989, p. 6.

49. André Berthol in Assemblée Nationale de la République Française, "Équipement militaire pour les années 1990–1993," 2e séance, 3 October 1989, pp. 3062–3063.

50. François Fillon in "Les Réactions [à la conférence de presse du Président]," *Le Monde*, 20 May 1989, p. 8. See also Assemblée Nationale de la République Française, *Avis présenté au nom de la commission de la défense nationale et des forces armées sur le projet de loi de finances pour 1990 (no. 895)*, Tome VII, Défense, Forces terrestres, No. 923, Opinion prepared by François Fillon, 9e Leg., le sess., 12 October 1989, pp. 11–12. See also François Fillon, "François Mitterrand a dégagé en touche," *Le Monde*, 26 May 1989, p. 2. (See also this chapter, note 11.)

51. See, for example, André Berthol (this chapter, note 49).

52. Boucheron, *Rapport*, p. 167.

53. Cohen, p. 22.

54. Le Prestre, "The Lessons of Cohabitation," p. 38. Le Prestre notes a tendency during cohabitation to "fear the consequences of conflict." See also Colomès and Chatenay.

55. Michel Rocard, testimony in Boucheron, *Rapport*, p. 721.

56. Jean Gatel in Assemblée Nationale de la République Française, "É-quipement militaire pour les années 1990–1993," le séance, 3 October 1989, p. 3040.

57. Le Prestre, "The Lessons of Cohabitation," p. 26.

58. During the Assembly's debate in October the opposition moved to censure the Socialists' proposed program law for 1990–1993 on the grounds that it was not a revision of the 1987–1991 law but rather a new law entirely. The debate in the Assembly, therefore, addressed both the current law and the proposed law. The motion to censure eventually failed, and the 1990–1993 law passed.

59. François Hollande in Assemblée Nationale de la République Française, "Équipement militaire pour les années 1990–1993," le séance, 3 October 1989, p. 3027. See also Boucheron, *Rapport*, p. 165.

60. Elie Marcuse and James Sarazin, "Défense: les vérités qu'on camoufle," *L'Express* (9 June 1989), p. 28.

61. Jacques Isnard, "210.3 milliards de francs pour l'équipement en 1990 et 1991," *Le Monde*, 25 May 1989, p. 14. And Michel Rocard, testimony in Boucheron, *Rapport*, p. 716.

62. Marcuse and Sarazin, p. 20.

63. Jacques Baumel in, Assemblée Nationale de la République Française, "Équipement militaire pour les années 1990–1993," 4e séance, 4 October 1989, p. 3077.

64. Marcel Duval, "The Prospects for Military Co-operation outside Europe: A French View," in Boyer, Lellouche, and Roper, eds., p. 69.

65. Cited in Boucheron, *Rapport*, pp. 336, 385.

66. Boucheron, *Rapport*, pp. 52, 74. See also Boucheron in Assemblée Nationale de la République Française, "Équipement militaire pour les années 1990–1993," le séance, 3 October 1989, p. 3026. Here Boucheron observes that "with its nuclear deterrent force and its power projection capability, France is the only European country with the means to carry out a credible foreign policy."

Benoit d'Aboville, a defense expert in the French Ministry of Foreign Affairs, also expressed his belief that an increasingly important issue for France beyond the year 2000 will be how to fulfill its Third World missions. He thinks public opinion will support the financing of forces for possible intervention in extra-European regions. (Interview with Benoit D'Aboville, French Consulate, New York, NY, 8 January 1990.)

67. Jean Lecanuet, "Le risque d'enlisement," *Le Monde*, 30 August 1990, p. 7.

68. Hassner, p. 77.

69. Huguette Bouchardeau in Assemblée Nationale de la République Fran-

çaise, "Équipement militaire pour les années 1990–1993," 4e séance, 4 October 1989, p. 3081.

See also Jolyon Howorth, "Consensus and Mythology: Security Alternatives in Post-Gaullist France," in Robert Aldrich and John Connell, eds., *France in World Politics* (London, Routledge, 1989), p. 31.

70. See, for example, The International Institute for Strategic Studies, *The Military Balance, 1989–1990* (London, Pergamon-Brassey's for IISS, 1989), p. 59. The number listed here is 292,500.

71. Yves Cuau, "Une armée de métier?" *L'Express* (9 June 1989), p. 29.

72. "Un sondage CSA pour *Le Monde* et FR 3," *Le Monde*, 23 May 1989, p. 14, questions 5, 8, and 9.

73. Hassner, p. 82.

74. This and following illustrations were related to me by a high-ranking American officer, formerly serving at SHAPE.

75. Hassner, p. 82.

CONCLUSION

This analysis began with a discussion of the inability of institutional inertia in NATO to withstand the accelerated pace of structural political change taking place in Europe today. The last chapter argued that the country in the strongest position to lay the foundation for a new security order in Europe, France, is unlikely to meet that challenge, precisely because of institutional inertia in its own national security policy. In fact, evolving internal and external pressures on France may even strengthen that inertia, ensuring that French initiatives in European security will remain in the realm of vague declaratory policy.

The American-led concept of tightly integrated security in Europe is waning, and the French-led concept of loose cooperation may never receive the focus and direction it would need to become an identifiable regime. Neither of the two main participants in the debate of the 1960s on the fundamental structure of European security is in an ideal position to assert its model. Even if the United States government had strong domestic support for continued engagement in Europe, if for no other reason than to protect economic links with the old continent, the American ability to compel European support for its vision of security would still be declining. On the other hand, while France's potential political leverage in Europe may be increasing, due in large part to the stability and strength of its contribution to security on the continent, its ability to rally active domestic support for an unambiguous leading

French role in European security is weakening.

The combination of a loosening inertia in NATO institutions and tightening resistance to change in French institutions should not imply a simple preservation of the *status quo* in European security. Certainly the momentum of arms control, popular revolution in Eastern and Central Europe, and German unification have ensured the inevitability of a fundamental transformation. The significance of relative inertias in NATO and France to that transformation is the loss of a focus to guide change. What the United States provided Europe through the institutions of NATO, in addition to the guarantees of extended deterrence and American participation in European defense, was a concrete direction, a blueprint for security. The Gaullist alternative, in theory, also provided a blueprint. Even if more loosely structured, the French concept established a definite set of principles in which to frame the construction of a European security regime. If the institutions built up through American guidance are faltering, and if France is unable to offer a new focus for fear of disrupting the balance between national and European imperatives, then from where will a new direction for European security emerge?

Helmut Schmidt's observation of 1987 that France is the only viable candidate for leadership of a new European security order is even more relevant today.[1] The expected American withdrawal, Germany's preoccupation with managing unification, Great Britain's tendency to remain aloof from the continent, and the lack of resources in the smaller countries sufficient to exercise a large degree of influence in Western Europe leave France as the one state best able to offer direction to Europe. "France, when it speaks clearly and looks ahead," observes Stanley Hoffmann, "can still say and do things that Germany, even unified and democratic, cannot take on for itself."[2] But with France constrained in its ability to fulfill that role, Europe will likely improvise through the current transformation. The coherence of the new order, which ideally would be visible during its construction, will instead be defined only with hindsight.

A "muddling through" is likely to characterize the near-term evolution of European security. This will mean a continued and perhaps even a relatively strong role for time-tested institutions. NATO is not apt to go away tomorrow, and its peacetime functions will probably be more extensive than a French-shaped regime might have envisioned. For instance, even if a formal structure is not set up, NATO could become, *de facto*, a major forum for arms control verification, consultation, and coordination. A strong role for NATO in the future as the "essential forum" for consultation among Allies was confirmed by Alliance foreign ministers in June 1991. While the Copenhagen conference was the occasion for acknowledging the potential for a common Western European security policy, the final communiqué preserved much of NATO's traditional functions.[3]

Although European liking for the American-led security framework that has prevailed since 1967 may be declining, from the 1950s up to the present day Europeans have consistently trusted the United States as the one Ally that would definitely come to their aid in a crisis. Trust among Europeans is considerably less.[4] The trust differential is demonstrated, for instance, each time NATO is called on to pick a new Supreme Allied Commander. Each time a SACEUR has retired, the idea of turning the office over to a European general has been discussed, but inevitably the only nation on which all sixteen can unanimously agree is the United States. Given a history of weak mutual trust, therefore, Europeans are not likely to let the Atlantic Alliance simply wither away, especially in the absence of a clear alternative.

At the same time, Europe will probably experiment with new roles for less active institutions. While lack of clear French leadership may impede ideas such as a renewed place for the Western European Union or more robust bilateral security relationships from moving substantially toward a coherent new order, other fora, most important the Conference on Security and Cooperation in Europe, will probably achieve new status. The CSCE process, as the one preexisting structure bringing together all 35 states (now 38, with the addition of the Baltic States) of the common European house, has the potential to serve as a testing ground for new, common, consultative activities, as launched in the Paris Charter of November 1990.

Moreover, elevation of an institution that emphasizes the importance of cooperation among independent states will benefit from strong French support. Even with weakened French leadership, a new concert of Europe is bound to incorporate some elements of the French model. Encouragement of the CSCE process would not risk domestic crisis in France, while it would promote at least one dimension of France's vision for future European security. A more robust, institutionalized CSCE will act as a check on reversion to a "bloc" mentality in both East and West.

In the improvisation that will define functions for new and old institutions, no single state will be able to dictate policy, and there will certainly be no preordained agenda. This vague process may, in fact, help to incorporate the Soviet Union and Eastern and Central Europe more fully into pan-European security. Absent a preconceived paradigm constructed in the West, those nations might feel less constrained in their participation. The fading of an American-led concept of the structure of European security and the probable failure of France to reassert a Gaullist concept would leave Europe a *tabula rasa*. There would be little if any fear of an overarching plan imposed by the West, and all nations might be more inclined to perceive themselves as equal partners in a common task than if an unambiguous French or American blueprint for security were initiated.

Although a French-led security order would be more loosely structured than an American-led security order, the former would still be distinctly western in nature. Gaullism evolved in a cold war environment; application of Gaullist tenets to a post–cold war system might be perceived as inhibiting a full transition to a new order. Also, as described in chapter three, in a French-led security order tensions with the American vision would linger, and this too might inhibit the construction of a concert of Europe. Thus, lack of direction from either the French or the American concept of security might, in the long term, lead to a more robust development of a pan-European system, unobstructed by vestiges of the Cold War.

Finally, the absence of clear, focused guidance, from France, the United States or elsewhere, may contribute generally to declining interest in military security in Europe. With the fading of the military threat on the continent and the end of the Cold War, policy-makers' attention will undoubtedly turn to other issues, such as the many challenges surrounding economic integration and more global dilemmas, for instance, the environment. Ultimately, France's failure to pave a new course for European security, rather than signal a return to the historical debate on the needs of defense, may instead hasten the emergence of new priorities for the European policy agenda.

NOTES

1. Helmut Schmidt, "Europe Should Begin to Assert Itself, and the French Should Take the Lead," article from *Die Zeit* translated in *World Press Review* (February 1987), p. 23.

2. Stanley Hoffmann, "La France dans le nouvel ordre européen," *Politique Etrangère* (no. 3, 1990), p. 511.

3. See extracts from the Copenhagen communiqué in "Les fonctions essentielles de l'Alliance," *Le Monde*, 10 June 1991, p. 3.

4. Stephen F. Szabo, *West European Public Perceptions of Security Issues: A Survey of Attitudes in France, the FRG, Great Britain, and Italy over Three Decades*, research report (Washington, DC: U.S. Information Agency, Office of Research, 1988), p. 25.

BIBLIOGRAPHY

ENGLISH LANGUAGE SOURCES

Books

Aldrich, Robert, and John Connell, eds. *France in World Politics*. London: Routledge, 1989.

Amme, Carl H., Jr. *NATO without France: A Strategic Appraisal*. Stanford: Stanford University Press, 1967.

Boyer, Yves, Pierre Lellouche, and John Roper, eds. *Franco-British Defence Cooperation*. London: Royal Institute of International Affairs, 1988.

Epstein, Joshua M. *Conventional Force Reductions: A Dynamic Assessment*. Washington, DC: The Brookings Institution, 1990.

Harrison, Michael M. *The Reluctant Ally: France and Atlantic Security*. Baltimore: The Johns Hopkins University Press, 1981.

Hobbs, David. *NATO and the New Technologies*. Lanham, MD: University Press of America, 1989.

The International Institute for Strategic Studies. *The Military Balance, 1989–1990*. London: Pergamon-Brassey's for IISS, 1989.

———. *The Military Balance, 1990–1991*. London: Pergamon-Brassey's for IISS, 1990.

Kissinger, Henry A. *The Troubled Partnership: A Re-appraisal of the Atlantic Alliance*. Garden City, NY: Doubleday & Company, Inc., 1966.

————. *A World Restored*. Gloucester, MA: Peter Smith, 1973.

Kohl, Wilfrid L. *French Nuclear Diplomacy*. Princeton: Princeton University Press, 1971.

Kolodziej, Edward A. *French International Policy under de Gaulle and Pompidou*. Ithaca, NY: Cornell University Press, 1974.

Laird, Robbin F. *France, the Soviet Union and the Nuclear Weapons Issue*. Boulder, CO: Westview Press, 1985.

————, ed. *French Security Policy from Independence to Interdependence*. Boulder, CO: Westview Press, 1986.

————, ed. *Strangers and Friends: The Franco-German Security Relationship*. London: Pinter Publishers, 1989.

Le Prestre, Philippe G., ed. *French Security Policy in a Disarming World*. Boulder, CO: Lynne Rienner Publishers, 1989.

Newhouse, John. *De Gaulle and the Anglo-Saxons*. New York: The Viking Press, 1970.

Office of Technology Assessment. *New Technology for NATO: Implementing Follow-on Forces Attack*. Washington, DC: Government Printing Office, 1987.

Rallo, Joseph C. *Defending Europe in the 1990s: The New Divide on High Technology*. London: Pinter Publishers, 1986.

Sloan, Stanley R., ed. *NATO in the 1990s*. Washington, DC: Pergamon-Brassey's, 1989.

Stromseth, Jane E. *The Origins of Flexible Response*. London: The MacMillan Press, 1988.

Yost, David S. *France and Conventional Defense in Central Europe*. Boulder, CO: Westview Press, 1985.

Articles

Alford, J. "The Place of British and French Nuclear Weapons in Arms Control," *International Affairs* (Autumn, 1983), pp. 569–74.

Apple, R. W., Jr. "In Washington, Just a Hint of the Alliance's Angst," *The New York Times*, 1 May 1989, p. A10.

————. "What Is Bush Up To?" *The New York Times*, 9 February 1990, p. A9.

Barre, Raymond. "Foundations for European Security and Cooperation," *Survival* (July/August 1987), pp. 291–300.

Berger, Peter. "French Defense Initiatives: Emergence of Second Pillar in NATO?" *Armed Forces Journal International* (August 1988).

Biden, Joseph R. "Bush, Not Kohl, Is Undermining NATO," *The New York Times*, 7 May 1989, sec. IV, p. 27.

Blaker, James, and Andrew Hamilton, "Assessing Military Balances: The

NATO Example." In John F. Reichart and Steven R. Sturm, eds. *American Defense Policy*, 5th ed. Baltimore: The Johns Hopkins University Press, 1982, pp. 333–50.

Boyer, Yves. "The U.S. Military Presence in Europe and French Security Policy." *The Washington Quarterly* (Spring, 1988), pp. 197–207.

"Britain to Cut Force in Germany by Half," *The New York Times*, 26 July 1990, p. A8.

Cody, Edward. "Angst over Germany Spreads to France," *The Washington Post*, 17 March 1990 p. A22.

"Comparison of CFE Declarations and Residual Ceilings," reprinted in *Survival* (January/February 1991), p. 83.

Drozdiak, William. "Paris and Bonn Want Gorbachev at G-7 Summit," *The International Herald Tribune*, 31 May 1991, pp. 1, 5.

Dumas, Roland. "One Germany—If Europe Agrees," *The New York Times*, 13 March 1990, p. A29.

"FAR from Perfect," *The Economist* (26 September 1987), p. 63.

Feld, Werner J. "International Implications of the Joint Franco-German Brigade," *Military Review* (February 1990), pp. 2–11.

Fenske, John. "France and the Strategic Defense Initiative: Speeding Up or Putting on the Brakes?" *International Affairs* (Spring, 1986), pp. 231–246.

Fitchett, Joseph. "Postwar U.S. Ascendancy Sidetracks Europe's Aspirations," *The International Herald Tribune*, 12 June 1991, pp. 1, 5.

"France Weighing Value of Political Autonomy against Trend toward Defense Cooperation," *Aviation Week and Space Technology* (12 October 1987), pp. 129–32.

Froman, Michael, Anthony Gardner, and Scott Mixer. "France and SDI," *The Army Quarterly and Defense Journal* (July 1987), pp. 299–304.

Gordon, Michael R. "Discount Soviet Peril to Iran, Cheney Tells His Strategists," *The New York Times*, 7 February 1990, p. A13.

———. "Pentagon Drafts Strategy for Post–Cold War World," *The New York Times*, 2 August 1990, pp. 1, 4.

———. "Reagan Arms Adviser Says Bush Is Wrong on Short-Range Missiles," *The New York Times*, 3 May 1989, p. A1.

———. "U.S. to Offer Soviets a Compromise for Cutting Aircraft in Europe Under New Treaty," *The New York Times*, 6 February 1990, p. A17.

Greenhouse, Steven. "Paris and Moscow Forging New Ties," *The New York Times*, 13 October 1988, p. A10.

Grosser, Alfred. "German Question, French Anxiety," *The New York Times*, 26 December 1989, p. A27.

Grove, Eric J. "Allied Nuclear Forces Complicate Negotiations," *Bulletin of the Atomic Scientists* (June/July 1986), pp. 18–23.

Howorth, Jolyon. "French Defense: Disarmament and Deterrence," *The World Today* (June 1988), pp. 103–106.

———. "Resources and Strategic Choices: French Defense Policy at the Crossroads," *The World Today* (May 1986), pp. 77–80.

Kupchan, Clifford A., and Charles A. Kupchan. "After NATO: Concert of Europe," *The New York Times*, 6 July 1990, p. A25.

Laird, Robbin F. "French Nuclear Forces in the 1980's and the 1990's," *Comparative Strategy* (vol. 4, no. 4, 1984), pp. 387–412.

Lewis, Anthony. "The Bush Disaster," *The New York Times*, 9 February 1990, p. A31.

Lewis, Flora. "America Could Leave the Pedestal Gracefully," *The International Herald Tribune*, 19 April 1991, p. 6.

Markham, James M. "On Disarming, France Opens a Door," *The New York Times*, 7 September 1988, p. A3.

———. "Soviet Bloc's Neighbors Seek a Grip on Unrest," *The New York Times*, 9 October 1988, sec. 4, p. 2.

Marsh, David. "Kohl Rejects Early Missile Replacement," *The Financial Times*, 10 February 1989, p. 18.

Mason, R. A. "Airpower in Conventional Arms Control," *Survival* (September/October 1989), pp. 397–413.

"Ménage à deux," *The Economist* (24 March 1990), p. 29.

Moïsi, Dominique. "French Foreign Policy: The Challenge of Adaptation," *Foreign Affairs* (Fall, 1988), pp. 151–164.

———. "Germany's Unity, Europe's Rebirth," *The New York Times*, 20 November 1989, p. A23.

"NATO's New Structure," *The Financial Times*, 30 May 1991, p. 18.

O'Boyle, Thomas F., and Philip Reyzin. "Nuclear Missile Talks Lend a New Urgency to Paris-Bonn Amity," *The Wall Street Journal*, 12 June 1987, pp. 1, 8.

Owen, David. "Anglo-French Nuclear Cooperation," *The World Today* (August/September 1985), pp. 158–61.

Riding, Alan. "Allies Reminded of Need for U.S. Shield," *The New York Times*, 12 August 1990, p. A14.

———. "Fear in Paris: Ties to Bonn Will Be Hurt," *The New York Times*, 9 November 1989, p. A13.

Rosenthal, Andrew. " 'War' Is Fought as Bush Looks On," *The New York Times*, 7 February 1990, p. A13.

Rudney, Robert. "Mitterrand Reelection Threatens Mobile S-4, *Hadès* Missiles," *Armed Forces Journal International* (July 1988), p. 32.

Schmemann, Serge. "The Tangle Thickens in Two Sets of East-West Talks," *The New York Times*, 29 November 1988, p. A8.

Schmidt, Helmut. "Europe Should Begin to Assert Itself, and the French Should Take the Lead." Translation in *World Press Review* (February 1987), pp. 21–23.

Schmitt, Eric. "Army is Paring Its Forces Despite Buildup in Gulf," *The New York Times*, 21 September 1990, p. A9.

Starr, Barbara. "Cold War Battle Orders Make Way for a New NATO Era," *Jane's Defense Weekly*, 8 June 1991, p. 961.

Westerlund, John S. "The French Army of the 1990s," *Military Review* (February 1990), pp. 37–47.

White, David. "NATO Plans Rapid Reaction Force Commanded by UK," *The Financial Times*, 31 May 1991, p. 1.

Yost, David S. "France in the New Europe," *Foreign Affairs* (Winter, 1990/91), pp. 107–28.

———. "Franco-German Defense Cooperation," *The Washington Quarterly* (Spring, 1988), pp. 173–95.

Papers, Dissertations, and So Forth

Bahr, Egon, Andreas von Bülow, and Karsten D. Voigt. *European Security 2000—A Comprehensive Concept for European Security from a Sozial-Demokratic Point of View*. Bonn: Presseservice der SPD, 1989.

Blackaby, Frank. *The "Comprehensive Concept" of Defense and Disarmament for NATO from Flexible Response to Mutual Defensive Superiority*. Washington, DC: The British American Security Information Council, 1989.

Davis, Paul K., Robert D. Howe, Richard L. Kugler, and William G. Wild, Jr. *Variables Affecting Central Region Stability: The "Operational Minimum" and Other Issues at Low Force Levels*. RAND Note, N-2976-USDP. Santa Monica: The RAND Corporation, 1989.

Duffield, John Stuart. "The Evolution of NATO's Conventional Force Posture." Ph.D. diss., Princeton University, 1989.

Gambles, Ian. *Prospects for West European Security Co-operation*. Adelphi Paper, 244. London: The International Institute for Strategic Studies, 1989.

Hunt, Kenneth. *NATO without France: The Military Implications*. Adelphi Paper, 32. London: The International Institute for Strategic Studies, December 1966.

Louvion, Lt. Col. Jean-François. *The French Rapid Action Force: A Key Element in European Conventional Defense*. Research report. Maxwell Air Force Base, AL: Air University, 1988. (NTIS, AD-A202 216.)

Morel, Benoit. "High-Tech, NATO, and Arms Control in Europe, a Case Study: Joint-STARS" Unpublished paper. Pittsburgh: Carnegie Mellon University, 1989.

Szabo, Stephen F. *West European Public Perceptions of Security Issues: A Survey of Attitudes in France, the FRG, Great Britain, and Italy over Three Decades*. Research report. Washington, DC: U.S. Information

Agency, Office of Research, July 1988.

Wendt, James C. *British and French Strategic Forces: Response Options to Soviet Ballistic Missile Defense.* RAND Paper, P-7188. Santa Monica: The RAND Corporation, March 1986.

Wendt, James C., and Peter A. Wilson. *Post-INF: Toward Multipolar Deterrence.* RAND Paper, P-7407. Santa Monica: The RAND Corporation, February 1988.

Yost, David S. *France's Deterrent Posture and Security in Europe—Part I: Capabilities and Doctrine.* Adelphi Paper, 194. London: The International Institute for Strategic Studies, 1984/85.

———. *France's Deterrent Posture and Security in Europe—Part II: Strategic and Arms Control Implications.* Adelphi Paper, 195. London: The International Institute for Strategic Studies, 1984/85.

Unpublished Historical Documents

All historical documents cited in notes with the notation "NSA" are available at The National Security Archive, 1755 Massachusetts Ave., NW, Suite 500, Washington, DC 20036. They are listed chronologically in a catalog published for the Nuclear History Program at NSA and are accessible to the public.

Acheson, Dean. *De Gaulle and force de frappe.* Memorandum. (20 February 1963). [Recipient not specified.]

Bohlen, Charles. U.S. Embassy, Paris. *De Gaulle's Position on MLF.* Telegram to U.S. Department of State (31 October 1964).

———. U.S. Embassy, Paris. *Meeting with Couve de Murville on MLF.* Telegram, to Secretary of State (19 November 1964).

Bundy, McGeorge (drafter). U.S. Department of State. *Discussions with Couve de Murville on MLF.* Telegram (2765) to Charles Bohlen and Thomas Finletter. U.S. Embassy, Paris (12 November 1964).

Drake, Waldo. "NATO Faces Necessity of Regrouping," *The Los Angeles Times,* 8 December 1957 p. 1.

Finletter, Thomas K. U.S. Embassy, Paris. *Conversation with French Permanent Representative to NATO, Seydoux.* Telegram (POLTO 595) to Secretary of State (19 October 1964).

———. U.S. Embassy, Paris. *NATO Force Planning.* Telegram (POLTO 713) to Secretary of State (26 November 1963).

Future of NATO. Position Paper for Kennedy-Macmillan Nassau Meeting, December 19–20, 1962 (13 December 1962).

Helms, Richard. Deputy Director for Plans, Central Intelligence Agency. *Views of President Charles de Gaulle regarding the United States, Europe and NATO; and Italian Reaction.* Memorandum to Director of Central Intelligence (18 March 1964).

Holifield, Chet. *Improving NATO Nuclear Weapon Planning*. Statement (3 May 1966).

Hughes, Thomas L. U.S. Department of State. Office of Intelligence and Research. *Review of Possible Modifications in the MLF to Take Account of West European Problems Revealed During the MLF Negotiations*. Research Memorandum to Secretary of State (28 October 1964).

———. U.S. Department of State. Office of Intelligence and Research. *Western European and Soviet Reactions to the Idea of a U.S.-German Bilateral MLF Agreement*. Intelligence note to Secretary of State (7 October 1964).

Mark, D. E. *Considerations involving Germany and France which Are Pertinent to Modifications of the U.S. Position on MLF*. White House Memorandum (4 November 1964).

McKillop, D. H. (drafter). U.S. Department of State. *Conversation between Ambassador Alphand and Secretary of State*. Telegram (733) to U.S. Embassy, Paris (23 October 1964).

———. (drafter). U.S. Department of State. *Meeting between Secretary of State Rusk and French Ambassador Alphand*. Telegram (924) to U.S. Embassy, Paris (15 November 1964).

Neumann, Robert G. *Political Consequences of Possible U.S. Aid to the French Nuclear Program in Exchange for France's Adherence to an Eventual Test Ban Treaty*. Memorandum to Mr. Schlesinger for the President (21 July 1963).

Newhouse, John. *Balancing the Risks in the MLF* (20 March 1964).

Norstad, Lauris. *NATO-French Problems*. Letter to President Dwight D. Eisenhower (20 April 1960).

Rostow, W. W. *The Coming Crunch in European Policy*. Memorandum to the Secretary of State (12 October 1964).

The U.S. and de Gaulle—The Past and the Future. Memorandum to the President (30 January 1963). [Author not indicated.]

U.S. Department of State. *NATO Political Consultations: The Harmel Exercise; French Withdrawal and NATO Counter-Measures; The Troop Problem and Burdensharing; U.S. Relations with NATO*. Administrative History (circa January 1969).

U.S. Embassy, Paris. *French Position on MLF*. Telegram to U.S. Department of State (7 October 1964).

———. *Meeting between de Gaulle and Rusk on MLF*. Telegram to U.S. Department of State (14 December 1964).

U.S. Mission to the European Communities, Brussels. *European Parliament Views on MLF*. Airgram (ECBUS A 399) to U.S. Embassies in Europe (2 December 1964).

U.S. Objectives in Europe and Recommended Strategy to Overcome Obstacles

Preventing the Attainment of U.S. Objectives (9 February 1963). [Author and agency origin not indicated. Probably U.S. Department of State.]

"Washington against a 'Third Force,' " Department of State translation of article in *Frankfurter Allgemeine* (28 July 1962).

Yount, Col. B. K. U.S. Department of Defense. Office of the Assistant Secretary of Defense for International Security Affairs, European Region. *Emergency Authority to Stockpile Atomic Weapons in France.* Memorandum for Vice President's Visit to Paris, 29–30 September 1961 (27 September 1961).

Published U.S. Government Documents

Baker, James A. III. *A New Europe, a New Atlanticism: Architecture for a New Era.* Address to the Berlin Press Club at the Steigenberger Hotel, Berlin, 12 December 1989. Current Policy, 1233. Washington, DC: U.S. Department of State. Bureau of Public Affairs, 1989.

U.S. Arms Control and Disarmament Agency. Office of Public Affairs. *CFE: Negotiation on Conventional Armed Forces in Europe.* Washington, DC: U.S. Arms Control and Disarmament Agency. Office of Public Affairs, 31 August 1990.

U.S. Congress. House. Committee on Foreign Affairs. Subcommittee on Europe and the Middle East. *Challenges to NATO's Consensus: West European Attitudes and U.S. Policy.* Report prepared by Foreign Affairs and National Defense Division, Congressional Research Service. 100th Cong., 1st Sess., 1987.

U.S. Congress. Senate. Combined Subcommittee of Foreign Relations and Armed Services Committees on the Subject of United States Troops in Europe. *United States Troops in Europe.* Hearing before the Combined Subcommittee of Foreign Relations and Armed Services Committees on the Subject of United States Troops in Europe. 90th Cong., 1st Sess., 26 April; 3 May 1967.

U.S. Congress. Senate. Combined Subcommittee of Foreign Relations and Armed Services Committees on the Subject of United States Troops in Europe. *United States Troops in Europe.* Report prepared by Mike Mansfield, Subcommittee Chairman. 90th Cong., 2d Sess., 1968.

U.S. Congress. Senate. Committee on Armed Services. Subcommittee on Conventional Forces and Alliance Defense. *Alliance and Defense Capabilities in Europe.* Hearing before the Subcommittee on Conventional Forces and Alliance Defense. 100th Cong., 1st Sess., 4 August; 7, 20 October; 3, 17 November 1987.

U.S. Department of State. *American Foreign Policy, 1950—1955, Vol. I.* Washington, DC: Government Printing Office, 1957. ["Articles of the

Western European Union," pp. 968–91. "The North Atlantic Treaty,"
4 April 1949, pp. 812–15. "Treaty of the European Defense Community," 27 May 1952, pp. 1107–1150.]

FRENCH LANGUAGE SOURCES

Books

Cohen, Samy. *La Monarchie nucléaire*. Paris: Hachette, 1986.
Hernu, Charles. *Défendre la paix*. Paris: J. C. Lattès, 1985.
Mitterrand, François. *Réflexions sur la politique extérieure de la France*. Paris:
     Fayard, 1986.

Articles

Citations with AGRA and AFP refer to French news wire services.
"Un accord à Vienne sur le désarmement n'apportera pas de changement à
     l'équipement des forces françaises," *Le Monde*, 2 February 1990,
     p. 3.
"L'allocution télévisé du Président de la République," *Le Monde*, 5 March
     1990, p. 6.
Amalric, Jacques. "Bonn fait une concession importante," *Le Monde*, 8 De-
     cember 1989, pp. 1–2.
———. "Un médiateur engagé," *Le Monde*, 20 May 1989, p. 3.
———. "M. Mitterrand souhaite sauvegarder tout le programme de défense,"
     Le Monde, 19 May 1989, p. 1.
———. "Les propositions de M. James Baker sur l'Europe suscitent à Paris
     satisfaction et perplexité," *Le Monde*, 15 December 1989, p. 3.
Balladur, Edouard. "Pour une nouvelle politique de défense," *Le Monde*, 6
     March 1991, p. 2.
Boucheron, Jean-Michel. "Accélérer le désarmement classique," *Le Monde*, 2
     December 1989, p. 2.
Bozo, Frédéric. "La France et l'OTAN: vers une nouvelle alliance," *Défense
     Nationale* (January 1991), pp. 19–33.
Brenner, Michael. "Une nouvelle optique sur la sécurité européene: le regard
     de Washington," *Politique Etrangère* (no. 3, 1990), pp. 543–57.
"La brigade franco-allemande a une valeur militaire réduite," *Le Monde*, 22
     April 1989, p. 6.
Chartier, Christian. "La Belgique et les Pays-Bas annoncent une réduction de

leurs troupes stationnées en RFA," *Le Monde*, 27 January 1990, p. 4.

Chaussebourg, Anne, and Alain Rollat. "M. François Mitterrand réplique à ses censeurs," *Le Monde*, 8 February 1991, p. 8.

"M. Chevènement en URSS: première visite d'un ministre français de la défense depuis 12 ans," AGRA, 2 April 1989.

Chevènement, Jean-Pierre. "La France et la sécurité de l'Europe," *Politique Etrangère* (no. 3, 1990), pp. 525–31.

"M. Chevènement laissera le premier ministre choisir les programmes d'armement à annuler ou à retarder," *Le Monde*, 26 April 1989, p. 11.

"M. Chevènement: 'Le missile Hadès peut être utile à l'Europe entière,' " *Le Monde*, 13 March 1990, p. 6.

"M. Chevènement: 'On ne peut pas se contenter d'une Europe à Douze," AGRA 1/1901, 3 January 1990.

"M. Chevènement plaide pour une 'identité européene' en matière de sécurité," *Le Monde*, 7 December 1989, p. 3.

"M. Chevènement plaide pour un système de sécurité collective en Europe," *Le Monde*, 5 June 1990, p. 7.

"M. Chirac favorable à des unités multinationales sous commandement européen," *Le Monde*, 25 May 1990, p. 7.

Chirac, Jacques. "Une remise en cause insidieuse de notre défense," *Le Monde*, 10 June 1989, pp. 1, 18.

"M. Chirac regrette d'avoir approuvé l'opération 'Daguet'," *Le Monde*, 4 October 1990, p. 9.

Colombani, Jean-Marie, and Jean-Yves Lhomeau. "Le sens d'un septennat," *Le Monde*, 16 November 1989, pp. 1, 10.

Colomès, Michel, and Philippe Chatenay. "Défense: ententes forcées," *Le Point* (7 March 1988), pp. 38–40.

"Le conférence de presse du Président de la République," *Le Monde*, 20 May 1989, pp. 2–7.

"Confiance et persévérance: Interview de Jean-Pierre chevènement, "*Armées d'Aujourd'hui* (February 1990), pp. 12–15.

Cuau, Yves. "Les français, doivent-ils avoir peur de l'Allemagne?" *L'Express* (16 March 1990), p. 40.

Cuau, Yves. "Une armée de métier?" *L'Express* (9 June 1989), p. 29.

De Bresson, Henri. " 'Il y a des moments où le silence est lourd d'ambiguités,' affirme M. Roland Dumas à Berlin-Ouest," *Le Monde*, 6 March 1990, p. 6.

"La déclaration commune [de MM. Kohl et Mitterrand]," *Le Monde*, 20 September 1990, p. 4.

De la Guérivière, Jean. "Le renforcement des compétences de l'OTAN et le rôle des Européens restent controversés," *Le Monde*, 20 December 1990, p. 28.

Delarue, Maurice. "Réponse à Jean-Paul Pigasse," *Le Monde*, 21 March 1990, p. 2.

Dhombres, Dominique. "Paris et Londres vont renforcer leur coopération en matière de défense," *Le Monde*, 7 May 1990, p. 4.

Dumoulin, Jérôme, and Sylvie Pierre-Brossolette. "Chevènement: la réunification n'est pas d'actualité," *L'Express* (24 November 1989), p. 30.

"M. Eyskens pour une Europe sous garantie militaire franco-britannique," AFP, 20 June 1989.

Fillon, François. "François Mitterrand a dégagé en touche," *Le Monde*, 26 May 1989, p. 2.

———. "Mais à quoi sert le 'Clemenceau'?" *Le Monde*, 8 September 1990, p. 2.

"Les fonctions essentielles de l'Alliance," *Le Monde*, 10 June 1991, p. 3.

"La France en faveur d'une défense Européene indépendante," AFP, 4 February 1990.

"La France n'entend pas baisser sa garde, assure M. Jean-Pierre Chevènement," *Le Monde*, 9 June 1989, p. 14.

"La France va créer un corps d'inspecteurs du désarmement," *Le Monde*, 13 January 1990, p. 10.

"MM. François Mitterrand et Helmut Kohl ont présidé la première réunion du conseil de défense et de sécurité," *Le Monde*, 22 April 1989, p. 6.

Gay, Pierre-Angel, Patrick Jarreau, and Eric Le Boucher. "Au colloque de république moderne, M. Chevènement se prononce pour une défense commune européene," *Le Monde*, 4 April 1989, p. 8.

"Le général Schmitt affirme qu'il ne faut pas confondre 'autonomie des forces' et 'autonomie de décision'," *Le Monde*, 21 November 1990, p. 4.

Giraud, André. "Construction européene et défense," *Politique Etrangère* (no. 3, 1990), pp. 513–24.

———. "Nos armes nucléaires," *Le Monde*, 16 January 1991, p. 2.

"M. Giscard d'Estaing souhaite 'une solidarité' franco-allemande en matière de défense," *Le Monde*, 3 April 1990, p. 3.

Gonin, Jean-Marc. "Paris-Bonn: fin de bail," *L'Express* (16 March 1990), pp. 44–46.

Hassner, Pierre. "Un chef-d'oeuvre en péril: le consensus français sur la défense," *Esprit* (March–April 1988), pp. 71–82.

Hoffmann, Stanley. "La France dans le nouvel ordre européen," *Politique Etrangère* (no. 3, 1990), pp. 503–12.

"L'intervention télévisée du Président de la République," *Le Monde*, 17 July 1990, p. 6.

Isnard, Jacques. "Une armée de terre sans ses missile nucléaires," *Le Monde*, 4 March 1989, p. 13.

———. "Un conseiller de M. Joxe plaide pour le maintien de la triade nucleaire," *Le Monde*, 19 June 1991, p. 12.

———. "Désaccord entre M. Rocard et M. Chevènement sur la programmation militaire," *Le Monde*, 25 April 1989, p. 16.

———. "210.3 milliards de francs pour l'équipement en 1990 et 1991," *Le Monde*, 25 May 1989, p. 14.

———. "Un entretien avec M. Chevènement," *Le Monde*, 13 July 1990, pp. 1, 9.

———. "La France, promesse d'une Europe de la défense," *Le Monde*, 14 July 1988, pp. 1, 11.

———. "Un héritage piégé," *Le Monde*, 29 April 1989, p. 14.

———. "M. Mitterrand devrait choisir entre un missile mobile et un système d'arme nucléaire adapté à l'avion Rafale," *Le Monde*, 16 January 1991, p. 16.

———. "M. Rocard assure que 'les principes de base' de la défense ne sont pas remis en question," *Le Monde*, 27 April 1989, p. 15.

———. "Vingt-neuf pays face à une forteresse," *Le Monde*, 16 January 1991, p. 4.

"M. Juppé (RPR): 'La France doit rester à l'écart de toute action militaire'," *Le Monde*, 8 November 1990, p. 40.

Kaiser, Karl, Laurence Martin, and Cesare Merlini. "La France devrait adherer au traité de non-prolifération," *Le Monde*, 3 June 1991, p. 2.

Le Bail, P.-Y. "Confiance et persévérance: interview de Jean-Pierre Chevènement," *Armées d'Aujourd'hui* (February 1990), pp. 12–15.

Lecanuet, Jean. "Ne devançons pas la musique!" *Le Monde*, 14 July 1990, p. 2.

———. "Le risque d'enlisement," *Le Monde*, 30 August 1990, p. 7.

Lellouche, Pierre. "Paris: deux logiques pour une stratégie." *Le Point* (7 March 1988), p. 39.

Lemaître, Philippe. "La France et l'Allemagne relancent le projet de politique étrangère et de défense européennes communes," *Le Monde*, 6 February 1991, p. 28.

"La lettre commune de MM. Kohl et Mitterrand," *Le Monde*, 10 December 1990, p. 4.

Lhomeau, Jean-Yves. "L'exercice solitaire de la décision," *Le Monde*, 22 January 1991, p. 13.

" 'La logique voudra que l'armée française stationée en Allemagne regagne son pays,' déclare M. Mitterrand," *Le Monde*, 9 July 1990, p. 5.

Marcuse, Elie, and James Sarazin. "Défense: les vérités qu'on camoufle." *L'Express* (9 June 1989), pp. 20–28.

"A Metz, l'état-major du 1er corps d'armée sera dissous," *Le Monde*, 22 June 1989, p. 12.

Ministère de la défense, service d'information et de relations publiques des armées. "Le Défense en Chiffres 1990, *"Armées d'Aujourd" hui,* supplément au no. 147 (February 1990).

"Paix et équilibre," *Armées d'Aujourd'hui* (February 1990), p. 8.

"Paris et Bonn souhaitent intensifier leur coopération en matière de défense et de désarmement," AFP, 20 April 1989.

Paris, Henri. "Les armées de l'an 2000." *Défense Nationale* (November 1989), pp. 31–42.

———. "Le défi interarmées." *Armées d'Aujourd'hui* (February 1990), pp. 17–19.

Pigasse, Jean-Paul. "La CED enfin!" *Le Monde,* 3 March 1990, p. 2.

Poirier, Lucien. "La greffe." *Défense Nationale* (April 1983), pp. 5–32.

"Les réactions [à la conférence de presse du Président]," *Le Monde,* 20 May 1989, p. 8.

"M. Rocard ironise sur la 'vaudeville' de l'opposition," *Le Monde,* 17 April 1989, p. 20.

"Le rôle de l'Europe en matière de défense," (extracts from final communiqué of NATO foreign ministers meeting, Copenhagen, 6–7 June 1991), *LeMonde,* 10 June 1991, p. 3.

Rovan, Joseph. "L'heure des deux unités," *Le Monde,* 2 March 1990, p. 2.

"Le RPR veut une seule Europe élargie aux pays de l'Est," *Le Monde,* 7 December 1990, p. 9.

"Un sondage CSA pour *Le Monde* et FR3," *Le Monde,* 23 May 1989, pp. 1, 14.

Tréan, Claire. "Calmer le jeu par le désarmement," *Le Monde,* 2 December 1989, p. 1.

———. "100,000 pièces à la casse," *Le Monde,* 20 November 1990, p. 3.

———. "MM. Dumas, Genscher et De Michelis prônent une accélération du processus du désarmement conventionnel," *Le Monde,* 27 January 1990, p. 4.

———. "MM. Kohl et Mitterrand relancent en commun la dynamique européenne," *Le Monde,* 10 December 1990, pp. 1, 4.

———. "Les modalités de la réunification de l'Allemagne détermineront l'avenir de l'OTAN," *Le Monde,* 7 February 1990, p. 6.

———. "L'OTAN reconnaît à l'Europe des Douze le droit de se doter d'une politique de sécurité," *Le Monde,* 10 June 1991, p. 3.

———. "Paris et Washington réduisent leurs divergences sur la défense," *Le Monde,* 8 June 1991, pp. 1, 8.

———. "Pour MM. Kohl et Mitterrand, le rattachement de la RDA devra renforcer le couple franco-allemand," *Le Monde,* 20 September 1990, p. 4.

———. "De l'utilité de ne pas s'entendre . . . ," *Le Monde,* 1 March 1989, p. 5.

Valentin, François. "Quelle défense pour quelle Europe?" *Politique Etrangère* (no. 3, 1990), pp. 533–41.

French Government Documents

Assemblée Nationale de la République Française. *Avis présenté au nom de la commission des affaires étrangères sur le projet de loi de finances pour 1990 (no. 895).* Tome XI, Défense. No. 922. Opinion prepared by Claude-Gérard Marcus. 9e Leg., le sess., 12 October 1989.

Assemblée Nationale de la République Française. *Avis présenté au nom de la commission de la défense nationale et des forces armées sur le projet de loi de finances pour 1990 (no. 895).* Tome VII, Défense, Forces terrestres. No. 923. Opinion prepared by François Fillon. 9e Leg., le sess., 12 October 1989.

Assemblée Nationale de la République Française. "Équipement militaire pour les années 1990–1993." Débats Parlementaires. *Journal officiel de la république française.* 9e Leg., le sess., 3, 4 October 1989.

Assemblée Nationale de la République Française. *Rapport fait au nom de la commission de la défense nationale et des forces armées sur le projet de loi de programmation (no. 432) relatif à l'équipement militaire pour les années 1987–1991.* No. 622. Report prepared by François Fillon. 8e Leg., 2e sess., 7 April 1987.

Assemblée Nationale de la République Française. *Rapport fait au nom de la commission de la défense nationale et des forces armées sur le projet de loi de programmation (no. 733) relatif à l'équipement militaire pour les années 1990–1993.* No. 897. Report prepared by Jean-Michel Boucheron. 9e Leg., le sess., 2 October 1989.

Chevènement, Jean-Pierre. *Allocution du ministre de la défense devant le centre des hautes études de l'armement, le 12 septembre 1989.* Diplo Paris, 21 September 1989.

———. *Discours du ministre de la défense devant l'assemblée de l'U.E.O., le 5 décembre 1989.* Bulletin d'Information, 7 December 1989.

Dumas, Roland. *Discours du ministre d'état à l'IHEDN, le 6 février 1990.* Bulletin d'Information. Diplo Paris, 7 February 1990.

Ministère de la Défense de la République Française. *Armées 2000.* Paris: Ministère de la Défense de la République Française, 26 July 1989.

Sénat de la République Française. *Avis présenté au nom de la commission des affaires étrangères, de la défense, et des forces armées, sur le projet de loi de finances pour 1990 considéré comme adopté par l'Assemblée Nationale aux termes de l'article 49, alinéa 3, de la Constitution.* Tome VI, Défense, Section forces terrestres. No. 62. Opinion prepared by Philippe de Gaulle. 9e Leg., le sess., 21 November 1989.

Other

Interviews: I have relied on information from four interviews with French and American civilian and military (active and retired) officials, held in January and February 1990. Where the information from those interviews is attributable, it is so cited in the text.

INDEX

About the Author

THEODORE ROBERT POSNER, a student at Yale University Law
School, is specializing in the study of security policy in Europe.